Paragliding

The complete guide

Paragliding
The complete guide

Noel Whittall

 The Lyons Press

Design by Krystyna Hewitt and White Line Publishing Services

Library of Congress Cataloging-in-Publication Data applied for.

Acknowledgements

Paragliding is packed with interesting and enthusiastic people, and without their help this book would not have been possible. I can only name a few, those who have given me particular help and encouragement:

BHPA: Tom Hardie, whose airspace expertise is second to none; and Mark Dale, who cannot be beaten on safety and technical matters.

The Whittall family: My sons Matthew and Rob, who are both at the top of the sport but who show remarkable patience concerning their aged father's flying; and Rosita Whittall for valuable help with the text.

Senior Instructor Eddie Close, who has the knack of making people learn without them realizing they have been taught.

Active Edge Paragliding (Yorkshire Dales): Dean Crosby; Tony Johnston

Eagle Quest Paragliding (Lake District): Gordon Oliver; Jocky Sanderson; Mark Sheffield

Mount Seven Paragliding Inc (Golden, BC, Canada): Eric Oddy

Peak Paragliding School (Derbyshire): Gerald Williams

Yorkshire Electricity: Terry Utley

The Met. Office: Jill Harmer

And all my many friends in the **Dales Hang Gliding and Paragliding Club.**

Contents

Introduction

Paragliders are so simple and so effective that they seem almost too good to be true. Just imagine: a personal aircraft that can be kept at the bottom of a wardrobe and transported in a rucksack, yet can climb in silence for thousands of feet and carry you for hundreds of kilometres. It is a sporting pilot's dream come true. I thought that I was lucky in the 1970s when I discovered the then-new sport of hang gliding. That seemed to be aviation reduced to the minimum. Little did I know that twenty years later I would find the same thrill again with even lighter equipment in the form of the paraglider.

Strictly speaking a paraglider is an aircraft which has no primary rigid structure, is capable of soaring flight and can be foot-launched from a hillside. Of course, that's not to say that you cannot tow-launch them too, if there are no hills handy.

At its most basic stage, paragliding is a bit like skiing: the run is exhilarating but ends up at the bottom of the hill. However, with a little skill the energy in the wind and the sun can be exploited to extend the run almost indefinitely. It takes time and patience to learn this craft of soaring, but the rewards of moving freely in the air make every moment worthwhile.

Having introduced the comparison with skiing, I am now going to move away from it very quickly. This is because it is so easy to think of a paraglider as just another piece of sporting equipment: after all, it costs about the same as a good set of golf clubs and doesn't

Facing page: *the author launching for a trial flight*

7

Units of measurement

Aviation units are an odd and inconsistent mixture. By international aviation convention, heights are generally measured in feet, horizontal distances in (kilo)metres or nautical miles, and speeds in knots (nautical miles per hour) — but records are given in kilometres per hour! Most of us think in miles per hour (mph) or kilometres per hour (kph), so use whatever you are comfortable with. Sport pilots in Europe tend to favour metres for height and metres per second for speed.

In this book I have used whichever units are most appropriate in the context, with equivalents where this would be helpful.

take up any more space. But the big difference is that it is an *aircraft* and must always be treated and used with the care and respect that all types of aircraft demand.

Airmanship

For me, airmanship is a way of thinking that adds up to safety for yourself and for everyone who may share the air with you. It's a basic attitude, a cast of mind. If you take up paragliding, airmanship is something which must be with you all the time. It means being able to appreciate the difference between taking a chance and seizing an opportunity. And then leaving *nothing* to chance.

The chapters in this book will lead you around many different areas of the sport, from the beginner stages to the challenges of soaring cross-country over serious mountains. I hope that it will show you what you can do and help you to develop the attitudes which will allow you to fulfil your own flying potential.

What no book can do is to teach you how to fly. That is a job for specially skilled instructors, and I cannot stress too highly the need to be taught at a paragliding school or club which is registered and approved by your country's paragliding governing body. In Great Britain this is the British Hang Gliding and Paragliding Association (BHPA). Addresses of governing bodies are given on page 197.

Where we came from

When you first see paragliding the activity seems so natural that it's hard to realize it hasn't been around for ages. After all, the apparatus is obviously closely related to a parachute, and stepping off a hill or casting free from a towline for the glide down is a lot less trouble than jumping from an aeroplane. Yet paragliders didn't really become generally available until the mid-1980s, since when growth and development have been rapid.

Several people contributed elements to the sport, starting in the 1940s, when Dr Francis Rogallo and his wife Gertrude were experimenting with unbraced kites at their family home near Harvard University. I love the tale of how the main passageway in their house was turned into an experimental wind-tunnel by running a fan at one end and closing the doors in certain combinations. The Rogallo experiments generated some very effective flexible kites, and eventually led others to produce the familiar triangular hang glider, complete with internal framework. The concept of the paraglider was within fingertip distance at that time, but the connection was never completed.

Meanwhile, jump parachutes were steadily getting better at handling and gained the glimmer of a glide performance. At first this was simply by removing sections of the rear of a circular canopy, so that it would be driven forward by reaction to the air rushing out during the descent. Then, in the very early 1960s, Pierre Lemoigne produced the designs which led to the Para Commander (PC) parachute, which has

Round-canopy parascending by the beach at Rio

numerous cutouts and slots, giving a greatly improved forward speed, good control, and the beginnings of a recognizable glide. Lemoigne's design was developed for *parascending* — being towed aloft by a line behind a vehicle — but soon became popular for jump parachutists too. This type is still in use, and the operators offering towed parascending flights behind boats at holiday locations often use derivatives of the PC. They are safe, stable and just right for that job.

Only a few years after the PC, parachuting took another step forward as far as canopy glide and control were concerned: in the USA Domina Jalbert patented his Parafoil, which introduced the concept of a double-surface rectangular-planform canopy formed from a number of airfoil-sectioned cells inflated by their passage through the air. This is often called the 'ram-air' system. The concept has not changed from that day to this, but the degree of refinement has been amazing. As an aside, in 1992 the paraglider manufacturer Trekking introduced a steerable reserve parachute for paragliders which bears a striking resemblance to Dr Rogallo's original kite designs.

We don't know the name of the very first paraglider pilot — it's probable that it was a parachute rigger who was trying out modifications on a sloping piece of ground — but we can be sure that the flights were short, because jump parachutes generally have a very poor glide performance.

In spite of the obvious similarities between the aircraft, there is a fundamental difference in attitude between parachutists and paraglider pilots. Most parachutists get the biggest satisfaction from the sensation of flight during free fall, and the journey after the canopy opens is a necessary inconvenience. Others are dedicated to developing landing-accuracy skills, in which the parachute becomes simply a delivery system. Airborne troops usually want the fastest survivable descent rate, because that means that they are hanging around as targets for as little time as possible. All in all, parachutes are about getting you down: paragliders are designed to keep you up!

Perhaps I should mention that paraglider pilots always inflate their wings before launching, unlike BASE (Buildings, Aerials, Spans, Earth) parachute jumpers who launch from suitable high points and then trust that their aircraft will assemble itself correctly on the way down. I understand why they do this, and don't have the hostile attitude to the activity that some sections of the aviation establishment tend to display, but I am content to obtain my adrenaline in more carefully measured doses.

Naturally, the first paragliders owed almost everything to parachuting technology, and they inherited the thick lines and other features that are essential to resist the considerable shock of repeated openings at very high speed. As soon as it was realized that hill-launching did not require the same strength margins, drag was reduced and performance improved dramatically.

*Parascending at the British National Accuracy
Championships in 1993. These canopies have
changed little from the jump type. They are not
suitable for hill soaring but still provide good
sport when used with a towline and a target.*

12

Lacking high, steep mountains, pioneers in Britain compensated by towing parachutists into the air under the high-performance canopies of the time. This developed into the activity of parascending, and thousands of ascents were made, tow-launched behind Land Rovers, with a very good safety record. The sport centred around airfields, with accuracy of landing being more important than duration of glide. Just one or two visionaries, led by Walter Neumark, could see the possibilities of soaring performance under canopies, and tried to develop it.

Parascending is still popular, and has spread to several other countries, often after being initially displayed as a sport by military personnel.

Paragliding is hang gliding's first cousin, and many of the personalities in the sport have also been active hang-glider pilots. My first contact came from Gerald Williams, a hang-glider pilot who became a lone pioneer, flying canopies in the Peak District of Derbyshire and trying to convince hang-glider pilots that this was something well worth getting into. Gerald was there, ahead of all of us, and he's still there, now instructing beginners with undiminished enthusiasm.

In Europe, three early starters were the flying adventurer and journalist Didier Favre, the innovative designer Laurent de Kalbermatten, and harness manufacturer Freddie Keller. They were flying canopies from the mountains around Mieussy, in the French Alps, in the late 1970s. By 1981 the sport had developed sufficiently for the Swiss to hold a championship at Wengen.

Internationally, the sport of paragliding operates under the benevolent eye of the Fédération Aéronautique Internationale (FAI), the world governing body of all air sports. The FAI's hang-gliding commission, the Commission Internationale du Vol Libre (CIVL), looks after the details, dealing with such matters as the allocation of championships and the promotion of safety standards. For sporting purposes paragliders have been

Gerald Williams helping a student in Derbyshire

given the category of Hang Gliders, Class 3. One of the first steps towards getting the sport firmly established and organized internationally came when Thomas Bosshard, then President of CIVL, demonstrated a parascending canopy to delegates at the 1986 CIVL meeting in Hungary.

A trial day at a training school is the ideal way to find out if the sport is for you.

Is it for you?

It is easy to find out if paragliding is for you: simply give it a try! You don't have to spend a lot on equipment, because the training club or school will supply everything in return for a reasonable daily fee which will include instruction. All you need is some suitable clothing — in Britain that generally means *warm* — and a good pair of boots.

People of both sexes and all ages take up the sport. You don't have to be super-fit, but you probably won't enjoy it much if you are really unfit. There will be a fair amount of walking up hills, and the ground-handling calls for some exertion — especially in the early days, when the wing always seems to be fighting you. In any case, if you suffer from heart problems or epilepsy, or any other medical condition which may cause difficulty, you should certainly consult your doctor first. Expect to be asked about health matters before you sign on at a training school.

Maybe you have already experienced the thrill of flying on a PC-type round canopy behind a boat on a holiday trip. That's a good initiation, but it's nothing to compare with the satisfaction of flying completely under your own control.

Piloting and drugs do not mix. Your instructors will not let you fly if you have consumed alcohol that day, or if they suspect that you have taken drugs.

Of course, not everyone who starts paragliding is new to aviation. You may have experience of sailplanes and

A tandem outfit in the Yorkshire Dales.

Dual flying needs special large paragliders, and the pilot must hold a dual rating. Be cautious about taking such flights with unregistered pilots in some countries.

light aircraft; or be a parachutist who wants to stay in the air for longer; or you may be one of the many hang-glider pilots who are attracted by the compactness of the equipment and so convert to canopy flying. Any experience of other forms of flying will be useful, but there will also be significant differences: you *must* have a fully qualified paragliding instructor.

My experience is almost entirely of launching myself from hillsides: for me this provides a degree of independence and freedom which I find particularly satisfying. However, in the absence of hills, tow-launching from flat fields is quite practical, but it must

Danger

I've put this under a separate heading, because I am so often asked 'Is it dangerous?' The short answer to this has to be 'yes' — potentially so, anyway. The only completely safe way of participating in sport aviation is to confine yourself to reading or dreaming about it. But, if you are prepared to learn paragliding properly, stick to the rules, respect the elements and understand your own limitations, the danger is very small indeed.

be performed with an experienced team, under controlled conditions, and from tow-sites approved by the aviation authorities. This book does not provide specific details about the techniques of towing, beyond warning explicitly against attempting to anchor one end of a line to the ground and trying to 'kite up' in the wind while tied to the other. This is an extremely risky practice which has cost lives.

Right and **above right:** *Each September a great festival of free flight is held in the French mountain resort of St Hilaire du Touvet. Enthusiasts and manufacturers vie with one another to produce the most ingenious paraglider-supported creation.*

Why it flies

The concept of the paraglider is wonderfully simple: a textile wing inflated by its own movement through the air, joined to a number of lines supporting the pilot's seat. The key words in that sentence are *wing* and *pilot*. Paragliders are *aircraft* which fly by using exactly the same aerodynamic effects that keep Jumbos full of paying passengers in the sky. However, unlike Jumbos, paragliders are very slow aircraft indeed — even compared with hang gliders, their nearest soaring relatives — and have only a small speed range.

We shall not delve very deeply into the world of aerodynamics, but it does help to think about the nature of the air and what happens when objects are moved through it. Fortunately the stuff is so plentiful that we normally take it for granted, but once you start flying paragliders you will find that you are suddenly much more aware of how it likes to behave. Think of air as a dense gas which isn't particularly keen to move, but which, if it has to, would prefer to travel in straight lines. Get used to the idea that it has considerable mass and reacts in predictable ways to being pushed, squeezed or dragged.

Another maxim that it's useful to keep in mind when considering how things fly, is that you don't get something for nothing. When you improve one area of performance, there is usually a price to pay in another area. For example, a small wing may fly relatively fast and handle well, but have rather a high sink rate. If the

*... a colourful but unruly mass
of fabric and line can transform
itself into a flying machine.*

wing is increased in size, the sink rate may improve,
but the top speed and easy-handling characteristics
will quite likely be reduced.

Keeping it in shape

I am still delighted by the way a colourful but unruly
mass of fabric and line can transform itself into a
stable wing without the help of any form of rigid
framework. That this wing can go on to develop
enough power to lift a pilot, is almost too good to be
true.

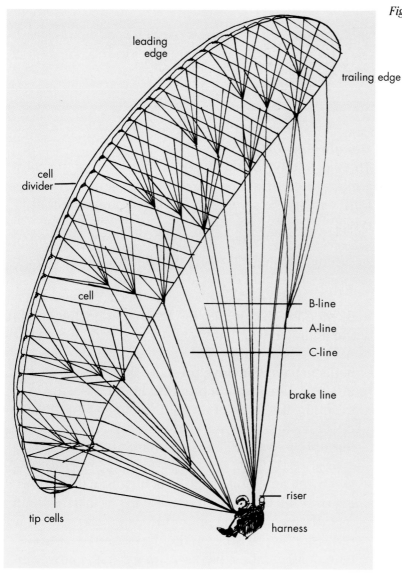

Figure 1 shows a typical paraglider. The wing is built up of many cells joined together side-by-side. The number of cells can be as low as about twelve for very simple wings, up to sixty or more for high-performance ones. Most of the cells have an opening at the leading edge which allows them to inflate, and the cell walls have holes cut in them to act as communication vents, allowing air to pass freely between the cells so that even pressure is maintained throughout the structure. The trailing edge is closed along its entire length.

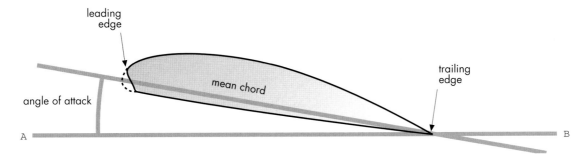

Figure 2: Airfoil section

leading edge

trailing edge

mean chord

angle of attack

A

B

Developing lift

The key to developing lift lies in the shape of the cell walls. These are shaped as shown in Figure 2, and perform exactly the same duty as ribs in a rigid aircraft wing.

Assuming that air is flowing past it from **A** to **B**, the airfoil generates lift in two ways:

- by meeting the air with the leading edge higher than the trailing edge. In this attitude the wing is said to have a positive angle of attack, and virtually any flattish shape will develop some lift if it is tilted in this way, because the pressure under the wing is raised by the force of the air pressing against it. This effect is often referred to as *plate lift*, and about one-third of the wing's lift is generated in this way.

- by having an airfoil shape which causes the air passing over the top surface of the wing to take a longer path than air passing under the wing. This causes a reduction in pressure on the upper surface. This type of lift can be called *section lift*. It is a powerful effect which normally contributes between 60 and 70 percent of the overall lift.

Figure 3: Airflow past an airfoil

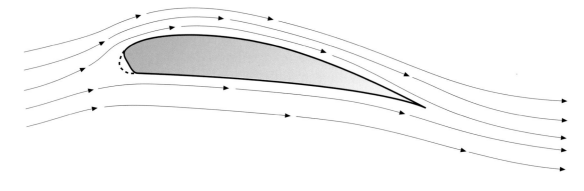

Inflation

A paraglider wing is held in shape by internal air pressure. The air is admitted through the ports at the front of the cells, and as long as these holes are clear and facing the airstream, the wing will keep its shape. The extra internal pressure is very low, but it's enough. Those gaps at the front of the cells look as if they would cause the development of a very inefficient airfoil shape, but it is not as bad as it appears: once the wing is fully inflated the air inside is virtually static, and there is a slight 'back-up' which causes a buffer effect at the leading edge. This allows a surprisingly smooth flow. At the front, the cell dividers are sometimes reinforced with a stiff plastic material called Mylar, to help in keeping the ports at the leading edge open at all times.The communication ports in the cell walls ensure that the air inside can flow from cell to cell across the wing quite freely, both when inflating it initially and during flight.

The ports at the front of the cells show up clearly in this shot of a basic training glider. You can also see the holes that allow the passage of air between the cells.

The array of lines connecting the wing to the pilot are fixed at points which have been very carefully calculated. The designer has to reconcile two conflicting requirements: there have to be lots of attachment points to keep the wing in an efficient shape when it is loaded, but because lines generate drag, which reduces performance, there need to be as few as possible. The end result is a very carefully balanced compromise.

The whole device depends on the weight of the pilot to match the other forces, so the position of the harness is absolutely critical. The lines are gathered together to join the harness via pairs of webbing straps called *risers*. On the simplest paragliders there will be two pairs of these. More advanced designs will have three or even four pairs. By convention the front pair are referred to as the A-risers, the next pair as the B-risers, and so on.

Within certain broad limits, as long as the air keeps flowing past the airfoil in an orderly manner, the pressure underneath will be higher than that above, and the wing will respond by trying to move upwards into the lower-pressure region. The upward force is *lift*, and can be measured in pounds or kilograms.

So far so good, but what keeps the wing moving through the air? It is obviously not being drawn through it by a propeller, so what does keep it moving along, and why does it stay up? The answer is gravity, and it doesn't really keep the paraglider up — it simply keeps it moving through the air in exactly the same way as it moves a skier downhill. While it is moving, the lift keeps the rate of descent low, but it is always there: gliders are always travelling downhill through the air. The only way they can really climb is by flying through air which is moving upwards faster than they are sinking. We deal with upward movement of air in detail in Chapters 6 and 7.

Drag

The lift is fine, but you don't get something for nothing. Here the price is drag, which comes in two forms. The first is *parasitic drag*. This is caused by the passage through the air of all the non-lifting parts of the glider. These include all the rigging lines, the risers, and of course the pilot. The main feature of parasitic drag is that, although it is small at low speeds, it very soon builds up as speed is increased. If you double the speed, you quadruple the amount of parasitic drag (in technical terms, the parasitic drag is proportional to the square of the speed).

The second form of drag is *induced drag*. This is drag which is induced by the passage of the wing itself through the air. It is a product of the way that the airfoil develops lift. We saw that the combination of the angle of attack and the airfoil section produces a higher pressure below the wing than above it, and it is this pressure difference that generates lift. However, because of the pressure difference, not all the air close to the edges of the underneath of the wing is content to stay on the same side — some of it naturally tries to migrate to the top, via the trailing edge and tips. Figure 4 gives a clearer idea of how this happens. This air movement causes turbulence around the tips and trailing edge, and this turbulence sets up drag.

The term 'parasitic drag' is a catch-all expression which includes several components, the greatest of which is *profile drag*. Keen pilots keep it to the minimum by sitting back in the harness in flight and by wearing closely fitting clothing.

Figure 4: Airflow around tips and trailing edge

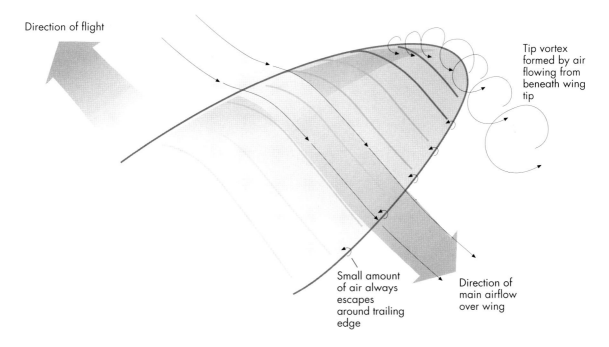

Direction of flight

Tip vortex formed by air flowing from beneath wing tip

Small amount of air always escapes around trailing edge

Direction of main airflow over wing

However, it's not all bad news: induced drag has the property of reducing with speed. This is because, when a glider goes faster, the effective angle of attack of the wing is reduced. You can think of this as allowing it to 'slice' through the air more cleanly, thus causing less disturbance and downwash, and so minimizing the induced drag.

To work out the total drag of the aircraft at any particular speed, the figures for the two types of drag are added together.

Lift, drag and the glide ratio

Figure 5 shows how the development of lift and drag relates to the speed at which the wing is flying. Note that total drag is lowest at the speed at which the two drag curves cross. This is the speed which will give the most efficient gliding performance for that particular wing. In the particular example shown in Figure 5, the lift is five times the drag at this speed. The point of interest in all this is that the ratio of lift to drag (l/d) also tells us what the gliding performance of the wing will be. The l/d ratio is effectively the same as the glide ratio, so in completely still air a paraglider with a best l/d of 5:1 will be capable of travelling forward 500 ft while descending only 100 ft. Needless to say, still air is

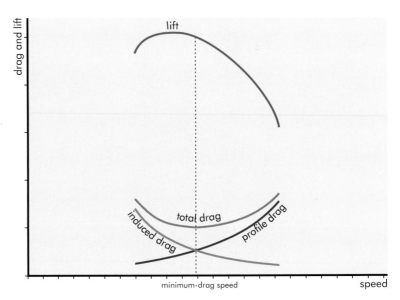

Figure 5: Lift and drag. The diagram shows in simplified form how the two types of drag alter with speed. When the combined drag is related to the overall lift developed by the wing, an impression of glide performance can be obtained.

rare indeed, as are the chances of flying at the optimum speed for the entire flight, but nevertheless l/d figures are useful as a general guide to performance.

Unfortunately, some manufacturers have tended to err on the side of optimism when advertising new paragliders, so it pays to treat published l/d figures with a certain caution.

Minimum sink

Just as there is a speed (the *maximum-glide speed* or *best-glide speed*) at which any aircraft gives its best glide ratio, there is another one at which the sink rate is at its lowest. This is rather unoriginally called the *minimum-sink speed*, which is frequently shortened to 'min-sink'. It is achieved at a high angle of attack, when the wing develops maximum lift. Consequently minimum sink occurs at the slow end of the overall speed range.

Stalling

The wing develops lift only while the airflow over it is fairly clean and undisturbed. Air will tolerate being forced to flow past an airfoil, changing its speed and direction slightly to accommodate it, but continuing to flow in fairly straight lines. However, if you ask it to deflect too far, it will react by refusing to follow the surfaces smoothly, changing instead to a broken, turbulent flow. When this happens, lift at once reduces dramatically, and the wing is said to be stalled.

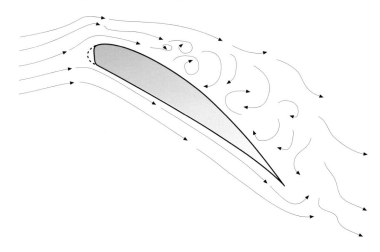

Figure 6: Airflow around a stalled wing

On a paraglider, stalling is usually experienced as quiet, smooth flight followed by a sudden rustling of the canopy which then swings back behind you and surges forward while you lose height *fast*. With paragliders, unlike other aircraft, the effect can be further complicated by loss of pressure inside the wing, causing it to change from its normal flight configuration. None of this is good news, and during flight stalling is something to understand but avoid. Contrary to what many people think, stalls can occur at *any* speed if the angle of attack is increased sufficiently, but certainly the most common stalls happen when pilots attempt to fly too slowly. In Chapter 10 we deal with stalls and recovery.

The polar curve

If you are new to paragliding, you can skip this section and come back to it later when you need to refresh your memory for your pilot exam.

The polar curve is a chart of the overall performance of your paraglider, plotting forward speed against rate of descent throughout its speed range. The axes of the graph are always drawn as shown in Figure 7. The minimum-stall speed and the effective top speed show clearly, and you can tell at a glance the rate of sink at any speed in the range. By drawing a line from the zero point (where the axes cross) to form a tangent to the curve, you find the maximum-glide speed. Further, you can work out the most efficient speed to fly in different headwind conditions by drawing a similar tangential line from the point on the speed axis corresponding to the wind speed. Frankly, you are unlikely to make much practical use of the information provided by a polar curve during your first couple of years of paragliding, but a basic understanding is a big help in appreciating the performance limitations of your aircraft.

Note that a published polar diagram describes the performance of the paraglider when supporting the ideal pilot weight — that is, the weight for which the glider

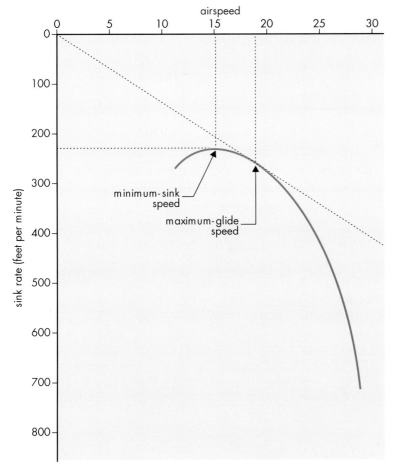

was designed. A lighter pilot has the effect of moving the whole curve up and left a little, while a heavier one moves it down and right.

The controls

Paragliders are different. The basic controls are simple, but they have no exact counterpart on fixed-wing aircraft; I suppose 'independent flaps' would be about as close as you could get to describing them in fixed-wing terms. They inherited the name 'brakes' from parachuting; although rather inaccurate, this expression is widely understood, so I have no qualms about using it throughout this book. One of the main skills to learn is to use the brakes smoothly at all times. Think of them as operating flexible guides for the air, not as machine-like levers or switches to be jerked on and off.

Your paraglider will be constructed so that if you sit comfortably in the harness and leave the controls alone it will fly in a straight line at around its best-glide speed. On beginner and intermediate models this will also be its effective top speed.

Speed is adjusted by using both brakes simultaneously: typically, completely off for best-glide speed; one-quarter to one-third on for minimum-sink speed, and fully on to produce a deliberate stall at the last moment for a light-wind landing.

When you look at a paraglider in flight, you will see how pulling the brakes causes the trailing edge to curve down. This increases the camber in the airfoil section, and also increases the effective angle of attack. Increasing the camber and angle in this way increases the lift, which explains why pulling the

Tim Taft gives an Apco Hi-Lite 3 just enough brake for comfortable soaring. Note how the trailing edge of the wing is pulled down a little on both sides. The Hi-Lite was a popular model in the early 1990s.

brakes a little helps you off the ground after a launch run. It also allows you to slow the glider down to its minimum-sink speed when trying to stay in rising air. There are limits: increasing the camber too much results in a stall.

Basic steering is accomplished by pulling down the brake on the side to which you want to turn. This causes an immediate increase in drag on that half of the wing, and the glider begins to turn. This is simple to do, and looks logical when you watch it happening, but the dynamics of the manoeuvre are quite complicated.

When you look at the brake lines, you will see that they fan out and are joined to the trailing edge at several points. This arrangement will have been carefully designed, and the safety and speed of turn will owe much to it.

Assuming that you start with both brakes on to some extent, tighter turns can be made by pulling further on one while easing up on the other. This should not be overdone: insensitive heaving on the brakes could lead to stalling the inside wing and starting a spin, or winding up into an ever-tightening spiral dive.

The brake lines show clearly as the control is pulled to make a right turn.

Matthew Whittall using brake and weightshift to turn his Firebird Barracuda. The way the brake moves the trailing edge shows very clearly in this shot of a high-performance model.

On most models you can assist steering by leaning in the direction of the turn. This is called *weightshifting*. Its effectiveness depends a lot on the design of the harness, and one which allows easy weightshifting may be a little too twitchy for beginners. This is a matter on which you will need expert advice from an instructor or coach.

There is more about turning skills in Chapter 3.

Roll and yaw

Because of the tremendous pendular stability provided by sitting several metres below the wing, paraglider pilots can be blissfully unaware of the effects of roll and yaw on their progress. Certainly these effects are not anything like as obvious as in other types of aircraft, but it is useful to recognize them.

Roll occurs when the wing is tilted sideways from the horizontal. Although some roll occurs when turning a paraglider, it is not the obvious effect with which pilots of more orthodox aircraft are familiar. The paraglider pilot needs only to be aware that the minimum-stall speed and the sink rate increase during roll, so any turns should be entered faster than the minimum-sink speed (see page 25).

Yaw occurs when the leading edge of the wing is not square on to the airstream. Turns involve an element of yaw, but because of the strong pendular stability the effect does not normally persist into level flight. You can observe yaw easily when on the ground: fly the paraglider like a kite by inflating the wing and gently turning it slightly to right or left and back again.

Adjusting speed

I have explained that a paraglider will normally fly 'hands off' at its most efficient glide speed, or thereabouts. Much of the time you will want to go slower than this to make the most of rising air, so you pull down the brakes to some extent on both sides. This slows you down by effectively increasing the angle of attack. You could achieve a similar result by pulling the rear risers, although this is not recommended because it would be easy to pull too far and stall the wing. (Useful to remember that you can use the rear risers this way in the unlikely event of a control line breaking.)

Increasing speed is another matter; you can make a slight improvement by putting your legs straight out in front of you and trying to keep drag to the minimum, but the only way to get a significant increase is by using a speed system. Designs differ in detail, but they almost all consist of a foot stirrup connected to the front risers via a simple pulley mechanism. Pushing on the stirrup shortens the front risers, so reducing the angle of attack and thus increasing speed. Some systems operate on both A- and B-risers. The effort required to push on the stirrup is surprisingly high, and the speed increase is not fantastic — sometimes it seems like a lot of hard work for an extra 10 kph (5 knots) at best, but when you feel you could be blown backwards over a spineback ridge, the effort is well worth it!

Preparing for launch. The stirrup for the speed system is tucked behind the pilot's legs until it is needed during the flight.

Because flying a high-drag aircraft at speed is a rather inefficient business (remember — the parasitic drag increases with the square of the speed), it is normal to use the speed system for short periods only. A speed system should never be fitted to a glider which is not designed for one, and they should not be brought into play in very turbulent conditions, as they do slightly increase the risk of the leading edge of the wing tucking under and closing the cells. Fortunately, it is an instinctive reaction to release the pressure on the stirrup if this starts to occur, so your safety should not be threatened.

Trimmers

Earlier generations of paragliders sometimes incorporated trimmers in the front or back risers. These were buckle-type arrangements which allowed adjustment during flight. They went out of fashion because of the difficulty of getting test certification throughout the adjustment range, but quick-release versions were reintroduced on several models, such as the Firebird 'Genesis'.

Harness

Paraglider harnesses can be very simple, consisting of little more than a wooden seat, a few strips of webbing and three buckles. The risers on the canopy are connected to the harness with a pair of maillons or karabiners.

Figure 8: Basic paragliding harness

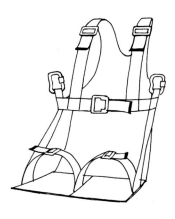

Figure 8 shows a typical harness of the type which you will probably use during training. It simply has to hold you securely in a position where you feel comfortable and from which you can reach the controls easily. Paraglider harnesses do not have to be adjusted as tightly as parachuting harnesses, which will come as good news to most males. That is not to say that they can be allowed to be slack, as that could allow the buckles to come undone in certain circumstances. When you are standing up before launch, the shoulder straps should be slightly too tight for comfort. You will then find that when you are seated in flight they will be just right. Most harnesses can be adjusted in flight

Paraglider design considerations

A modern paraglider is a wonderful example of practical design. You can pull it up off the ground to inflate it in nil wind, stabilize it overhead with a touch of the brakes, launch it at a steady trot, and yet it will also fly forwards in quite a strong breeze. It turns with a gentle pull on a single handle, or will fly straight with little more than an occasional shift of your shoulders. This is all because of intensive development. The easy inflation is due to a combination of the choice of airfoil section, the size and shape of the cell openings, the positions of the lines, the lengths of the risers and the layout of the brakes. It can do all this and still comply with the requirements of the certification programmes.

Now, imagine that the manufacturer's sales office demands that the model should have a higher top speed. Simple! Just cut down the area of the front openings a little and shorten the front lines to give a slightly lower angle of attack. Result: more speed; but now the wing has become a pig to inflate on the ground and is more prone to spinning if handled roughly in the air. A whole new development programme is needed to get the old easy-handling characteristics back into the faster wing. This illustrates the way that paraglider design is a constant matter of compromise.

The Edel design team discussing modifications during a pause in testing: Rob Whittall (left), Gin Seok Song (centre) and Kaoru Ougisawa (right)

quite easily, but this is not something you will be wanting to do until you have an hour or two of airtime.

Because walking in a harness which is correctly adjusted for flight is not particularly comfortable, it is not uncommon to release the leg straps to avoid the Quasimodo-stoop effect. Unfortunately this can be fatal, as it is all too easy to forget to secure them again. This usually happens when you have already made one flight and decide to release the straps for the walk back for another. I own up to having done this, and fortunately I got away with it. I have seen others do it too, so be aware of the hazard and **make your pre-flight check every time!** The next chapter tells you what to check.

Laurent de Kalbermatten's elegant Magistair was an attempt to obtain high performance through using a very narrow wing. A transverse flexible batten helped to hold the shape. The model did not go into production.

34

Practical piloting

At the risk of repeating myself, I stress that this chapter, like the rest of the book, is not intended to replace the services of instructors. Paragliding is not a teach-yourself activity.

In the descriptions I have assumed that the paraglider has a three-riser layout. If a two-riser system is in use, ignore the references to C-risers.

Ground-handling in easy conditions

It is far easier to handle a paraglider in the air than on the ground. This thought may be a comfort after you have spent an hour or so wrestling with an undisciplined wing at the start of your training course. Unfortunately, you have to learn ground-handling skills before you can proceed into the air, and the more practice you can get, the better. The ideal conditions in which to learn are plenty of open space and steady light winds of up to 10 mph (16 kph). You do not have to be on a hill — in fact it is better if you are not. In this wind strength the paraglider wing will lift itself quite easily, but you should not have any trouble anchoring it by yourself.

Pre-flight checks

Pre-flight checking must be a basic part of your flying from the very beginning. It is not something to do when you feel like it — do it every time. Good pre-flighting saves lives, usually your own.

Equipment inspection — at the start of each day and routinely throughout the day

1 **Canopy**: Correct size for pilot. All stitching sound. No broken or frayed lines. No obvious kinks.

2 **Harness**: Good condition, with no fraying of webbing or stitching. Buckles correctly fitted and secure.

3 **Riser attachments** (maillons or karabiners): If steel — no rust. If alloy — no deep scratches. Fitted to harness so that the screws are inboard.

4 **Brake lines**: Handles firmly attached (use bowlines and tape the loose ends for extra security) and no obvious wear, particularly where the lines pass through guides or pulleys on the risers.

5 **Helmet**: Correct size and in good condition.

Pre-launch checks — every time

1 Helmet on and fastened?

2 Harness on and all straps secure?

3 Lines and risers free and untangled?

4 Maillons/karabiners screwed shut?

5 Speed system (if fitted) connected?

6 Brake lines free and in the correct hands?

7 All clear above and behind?

8 Wing: all cells inflated and under control?

9 All clear in front?

Launch!

In-flight checks

Develop the habit of having a good look round the harness and canopy from time to time once airborne. A line broken by snagging on a rock during inflation is easily missed on the ground but will be obvious in flight. Check that karabiners are correctly aligned too. If the glider is not 100 percent, make a safe landing at the earliest opportunity.

Canopy inspections

At least annually (and I like to do it far more often) your canopy must be given a thorough inspection. This should be a cell-by-cell going-over, looking for worn areas and strained or broken stitching. It is also a good time to delve into it and remove any grass seeds, bits of twig or any other foreign bodies that will have found their way aboard. Run all the lines through your fingers, feeling for kinks or breaks, and check all their terminations.

Line lengths are critical, and certain line materials can stretch significantly during an active flying season. Your glider's handbook should include a measurement chart of all the lines so that you can check them accurately.

If there are bleached areas or other evidence of discoloration, have the canopy checked by a respected dealer who will ensure that it has not become weakened by exposure to ultraviolet radiation or dangerous to fly because of porosity.

A first-day student builds a wall while the instructor demonstrates. Students often act as anchor people for each other until they have become used to controlling the power of the wing in even a light breeze.

Building the wall — a light-wind exercise

A typical exercise starts with the wing lying on its back with the wind blowing towards the trailing edge. The harness is laid out in front of the trailing edge. With helmet on, you clip in to the harness and take up the reverse launch position which will soon become very

A perfect low wall formed with a Firebird Apache

familiar. Identify the front risers and use them to tease the A-lines up a little. The wing will immediately come to life as air enters the cells and it will take on the form of a wall. Forming and controlling this wall shape is a basic skill which you will use every time you launch in anything but the lightest winds. Practise raising and lowering the wall by pulling the front risers by hand, and then by simply leaning backwards and forwards so that your body does the work. See how the wall drops as soon as you let the tension off the A-lines. At this stage don't let the wall get higher than about a metre (3 ft). As soon as it looks like growing too high, move towards it to take the pressure off.

Above left and above: The wall is raised and lowered simply by pulling both front risers.

Next, take hold of the brakes, either by the handles or alternatively by the lines themselves, leaving the handles attached to their risers. Again raise and lower the wall, this time using a pull on both brakes together to help lower it.

A stable wall established with a prototype Genesis during trials

Full inflation
The next stage is to 'fly' the wing above your head like a giant stunt kite. Check that your back is completely into the wind, and then — smoothly and fairly slowly — guide the front risers up, using your body weight pressing into the harness to help, and letting go of the risers just before the wing reaches full height.

If you are very lucky it will stabilize directly overhead, leaving you to marvel at the size and shape of it. More likely, it will fall off to one side, trying to take you with it; or it will overshoot, collapse, and engulf you in a sea of nylon. After a few more attempts, during which the instructor will disentangle you each time, you will begin to get the feel of it. Soon you will have learned to move sideways as necessary to keep under the centre of the arc of the wing, simultaneously applying some brake on the side you are moving away from. You will also sense when to use a touch of both brakes together to stop it all overtaking you. If the wind is steady you will be able to keep the wing up for minutes on end.

Figure 9: Move to keep yourself in the centre of the arc of the canopy, applying just a dab of brake as necessary.

Below: *With a bit of practice you will be able to run forward with this sort of commitment, while using the minimum of brake needed to retain control.*

Turn and run

The next ground exercise is to practise turning so that not only is the wing facing into the wind, but you, the pilot, are too. Simply turning around to take the half-twist out of the risers is easy, but problems arise because of the need to swap hands on the brakes. No matter how you do this, there is likely to be a second or so when you have no effective control. Ideally, you want to walk backwards into the wind while turning, simultaneously looking up at the wing and juggling the brake handles. This does not always go entirely smoothly at first.

Once everything is stabilized and facing in the right direction, lean forwards, make sure that there is no tension on the brakes, and run powerfully forwards. When you can manage all this without too much

drama, you are almost ready to move on to a training hill for your first launches.

Collapsing the canopy

By now you will be itching to get off the ground, but there is one more exercise to master first: collapsing the wing when you want to. In the light winds you should be training in, this is very easy, but the lessons learned now will be vital the first time you find yourself touching down in a brisk breeze.

If you are using a basic training glider with just two risers on each side, the positive way to collapse it is to pull down firmly and confidently on both rear risers simultaneously. The wing will disappear behind you and expire onto the ground. As it does this, you must turn and run towards it so that the lines stay slack. Keep hold of the rear risers, and take care that the front ones are given no opportunity to tighten.

In light winds the same technique can be used on a three-riser wing, but you should also learn to collapse it by pulling strongly on the middle risers. You will hear this called 'B-lining', and it is the safest way of collapsing many paragliders if the wind is strong. As long as the B-lines are kept tight while all the others are slack, the wing will be safe, although it may flap around a lot.

Once you have collapsed the wing, keep hold of the risers you used to cause the collapse until you have moved around the wing and are certain that it really is completely under control.

There are other ways of collapsing a wing, some of which are peculiar to certain gliders. Be guided by your instructor in such cases.

The forward launch

There are two main ways of launching a paraglider, and the forward method is the one you usually start with. You will also hear it called the alpine or snatch launch. In very light or nil-wind conditions it is the only method which works, but if there is a blow of more than 5–6 mph (8–10 kph) I prefer the reverse method (see page 48).

For a forward launch, lay the wing out on its back, with the trailing edge towards the launch direction: the

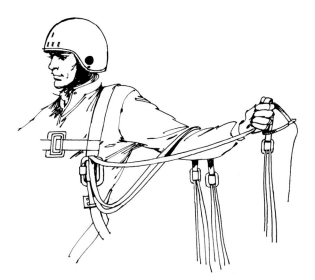

Figure 10: Always take care to route the risers over your arms correctly when making a forward launch. Note how the front risers (the As) are held in the hands while the others pass freely over the forearms.

launch will be cleaner if the wing is laid out in the form of a very shallow bow, with the tips slightly forward of the centre. Then spend a bit of time making sure that the lines are free of snags, lead them forwards, and clip yourself in. Make another careful check that the risers are not twisted by lifting them up and looking back along each in turn. Lead the B- and C-risers over your forearms, and take hold of the brakes and front risers (see Figure 10).

Left *and* **below:** *Forward launch in light wind. The arms should move in an arc so that they follow the lines up as smoothly as possible.*

At this stage it is useful to spread your arms and very gently pull on the front risers so that you can tell that the tension on each is identical. This ensures that you are correctly centred relative to the wing.

All OK? Take a pace backwards, keep your arms spread and move forwards powerfully but without snatching. Try to bend forwards slightly from the waist during all this. The first pace should be quite slow — just a walk really — which starts the inflation. Until the wing is overhead and you have let go of the front risers, you won't need to be going quickly. As it goes overhead, you will probably need to use both brakes a bit to stop it overshooting. Once it really is up, and preferably after you have managed a glance at it to check that all the cells are inflated, lean forwards into the take-off run, keeping your arms well back, and somehow managing to take another upward glance to ensure that the canopy is indeed fully developed. After a few paces, a gentle application of the brakes to increase the angle of attack should complete the launch.

That's the theory, anyway. Like most of us, I can get it wrong in many ways. I can snatch the start so that control is lost immediately; I can bring my arms forward too soon (and usually do); I can get the wing up so fast that it shoots forwards and collapses; I can hesitate and let it collapse by default; I can hold pressure on the front risers too long; I can forget to look up, and so on. At some stage you will probably develop your own variations. But when the rhythm is just right and a virtually effortless smooth launch results, the satisfaction is great.

Ground-handling in a wind

Sooner or later you will want to inflate your wing in a moderately strong wind, and this can be a rather frightening procedure for beginners. I learned the hard way, at the expense of some bruises and grass stains (and worse) on knees and elbows. Here are some tips which should take some of the pain and fear out of the operation.

Always put your helmet on and secure it before clipping into the harness.

Lay out the wing on its back, as for the forward launch. Set it out square-on to the wind, which will not necessarily be coming straight up the hill; don't worry too much about the outer parts and tips, as long as the centre cells are clear and unobstructed. If the harness is attached, ensure that you keep it fairly close to the trailing edge of the wing, so that there is no chance of the front lines becoming just taut enough to open a cell or two — it doesn't take much.

With one hand, take hold of both the brake lines about an arm's length above the handles and *keep* hold of them there. At this stage leave the handles attached to the studs on the risers. Now lift one complete set of risers over your head and make a half-turn so that you are facing the wing. Keep some slack in all the lines except the brake lines, and don't worry if the wing is flapping around a bit — as long as you keep hold of the brakes it will not get away from you.

Keeping hold of the lines as described above, also get hold of the brake handles and remove them from their studs. Sounds tricky, but it's not difficult when you try. At this learning stage it will be easiest if you hold the brake controls so that the left and right hands pull the corresponding left and right brakes as you look at them now. Then pay out the brakes progressively until you have hold of the handles only. You will need to have your arms almost straight out behind you now to keep control of that trailing edge.

Move backwards gingerly and the cells will start to inflate. Get the middle of the wing inflated to form a shallow wall, maybe 2 ft (600 mm) high. If you have difficulty doing this, it is probably because you are pulling the brake lines too far, so let them go out a little. Practise carefully altering the height of the wall at this stage. The A-lines will be just taut, and if you lean your shoulders back a little while *easing* out on the brakes, the wall will build higher. You will find that the outer cells on either side will now inflate of their own accord. Don't snatch at the controls, ease them, and make everything happen at your speed.

If one tip inflates and the other is reluctant, it may be because the wing is not quite square-on to the wind. Try pulling the fully-inflated side towards you, controlling its wall height with the brake, while you move across towards the uninflated tip. This will usually do the trick.

Spend quite a bit of time getting the feel of the wing under these conditions. This type of control is essential if you are to use either of the reverse-launch methods successfully. If things seem to be getting out of hand, move towards the wing; the leading edge will drop as the pressure comes off the A-lines, and simultaneously

Rob inflating a Navaho in a brisk breeze

you pull the brakes on more to keep it down. Wind the brake lines round your hands if need be ('taking wraps'). The great temptation when handling in a wind is to do everything in a rush, whereas you need control and balance. Take time to experience how a pull on the left or right brake affects the wall: you have lots of control as long as you keep your head and do the correct things.

If you really do get everything wrong, there are two accepted ways of minimizing the drama:

1 Haul one brake line right in and completely release the other. Keep hauling, hand over hand. The wing will flail around a lot, but at least you should not experience too much of a cross-country drag.

2 Pull one or both of the rear risers (the C-risers, assuming the glider has a three-riser layout) really hard and keep on pulling.

If you can, move towards the canopy as soon as possible — your aim is to keep the front risers slack at all costs. If you can dash around one side of the wing, so much the better.

If you are past the point of no return and are being dragged face-down across the field, accumulating evidence of the livestock that was there before you, then option 1 is the only practical remedy. Whatever you do, try to avoid the situation where the glider rotates and flies hard into the ground with a whump! This puts shock pressures into the cells and has been known to burst seams. It is often caused by pulling one brake on an unstabilized canopy without fully releasing the other.

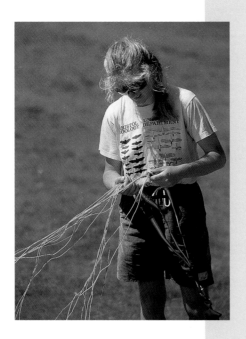

Tangles

Sometimes the lines will seem to be hopelessly tangled when you try to lay the paraglider out. If this is the case, don't panic, and don't immediately start undoing maillons. Take stock of the situation, and if there is somebody else who can help, don't be too proud to ask. The most common fault is that both sets of risers are twisted, and all that is needed is for the harness to make a forward or backward somersault to clear the problem. Whether you remain in it while this is done is a matter of personal taste.

If you have a really bad tangle, try to get the glider out of the wind and sort it out methodically. At most you may need to unhook the harness from the risers — never more than that. It is amazing how the most hopeless-looking bird's nests can be cleared in one or two moves with two people and a little patience.

Reverse launching (initial training method)

The forward launch is simple in very light wind conditions, but you can't consider yourself a real paraglider pilot until you have mastered the reverse launch. The ground-handling procedure described in the previous section prepares you for the simple reverse launch which is used in stronger winds. You can use it whenever the breeze is strong enough to inflate the wing without you having to pull it forwards. It is a more complicated procedure than the forward method, but there are two main reasons for it: it allows you to use your body weight effectively for control in stronger winds, and it lets you observe the wing throughout all stages of inflation.

Before we get into the details of the technique, there are two good habits you should try to develop:

- **Try always to turn in the same direction.**
  It doesn't matter which way this is, choose whichever feels natural at the start and stick to it from
  then on. This will reduce the likelihood of finding
  that you have put an extra turn into the rigging
  when you take off, instead of removing the half-
  turn that will inevitably be there. Mark Dale
  suggests a very simple dodge for deciding which
  way you will have to turn: simply check which riser
  is on top, and remember that the shoulder it goes
  to will have to turn backwards. I normally lift the
  left risers over my head at the start and therefore
  turn left to take off. Think about it and decide
  which way feels most natural for you. If you have
  put a twist into the risers when dropping the
  canopy on the previous flight, you may find that
  your usual turn direction will only make things
  worse. Develop the habit of checking for this as a
  routine part of your pre-flight procedures.

- **Always wear gloves.** You will have to pull on the
  brake lines at points well above the handles, and it
  is very easy to give your fingers painful friction burns
  if the lines are whipped through them by an unexpected gust.

Now for the technique, which is almost a replay of the
ground-handling exercise in a fresh wind. We'll
assume that you are on a smooth ridge with a wind of
about 12 mph (20 kph) blowing straight on.

1 You have made sure that there is plenty of clear
  space around you — especially in the all-important
  drag-back area directly downwind. With harness
  and wing carefully checked, and the wing laid out
  across the wind, build a low wall (see page 38).

2 When you have the wing nicely stabilized in the
  wall, check your footing — one leg forwards, the
  other back — and grasp the front risers just below
  where they meet the lines.

Reverse inflation. Notice how the student leans well back into the harness at the start so that her body is contributing to the pull-up. As the canopy comes overhead, she is ready to steady it with the brakes.

3 Pull the risers with a confident steady pull, aiming to keep your arms straight and in line with the risers as the wing comes up. Don't snatch! Take a step or two towards the wing as this happens (you probably won't have much choice) and be ready to apply some brake to keep it stabilized directly overhead.

4 Once the wing is stable and you are satisfied that no lines are snagged, make a half-turn, change over the brake handles into the correct hands, and launch.

That is exactly what is supposed to happen, and it usually does, but you will also encounter some involuntary variations. The most popular of these is to find that what you thought was a 10–12 mph wind (17–20 kph), is actually a bit stronger. You get the wing inflated OK, but the second it is overhead you are whisked off the ground without having much say in the matter and with the lines still crossed. Obviously this is something to avoid, but it will happen to you sooner or later. The big thing is not to panic; the pull on the lines will automatically rotate your harness into the correct direction, and you get on with piloting as if nothing untoward has happened. A slight complication will be that you have to get your hands onto the appropriate brake handles at some time during the procedure, which is why I like the continuous-control method which is described next.

It happens to the best! Rob sorting out the brakes during a windy launch in Japan

Reverse launching (continuous-control method)

This is a simple variation of the previous method, and I am glad to see that the training schools are taking a greater interest in it now. The only difference is that you take hold of the brake handles as they will be when you are flying. This has the great benefit of not requiring you to shuffle the handles from one hand to the other when you launch, so you have full control at every stage of the operation. However, there is a price to pay: as you build the wall, you will find that your right hand controls the left wing, as you look at it, and vice versa. This does take a bit of getting used to, but I think the effort is well worth it. Spend some time ground-handling on the flat before trying this in anger on the hill.

I think that this continuous-control system is beneficial when reverse launching in all conditions. It is particularly useful in lightish breezes, when you often see wings collapsing because the pilot doesn't keep control while swapping handles.

Flying straight

French team pilot Olivier Tops flying straight out from the hill. No brake is being used at this stage.

A correctly trimmed paraglider will fly straight in calm air without any help from the pilot. However, air is rarely calm, so you will need to give it a little help by applying pressure to the appropriate brake from time to time. These corrections should be very smooth and gentle: just small movements which allow plenty of time for the wing to respond. At first you will probably tend to over-control, because paragliders react much more slowly than, say, cars or bikes.

You will have been taught to cruise with a small amount of brake applied — on most training gliders this will be equal to about a hand's width. This is a useful guide, but don't let yourself get into the habit of thinking in terms of position alone when it comes to applying brake — feel is more important. Try to develop a feeling for the tension on the brake lines, and keep it equal. If you run into lumpy air, let your hands move a little to counter the movements of the wing. For example, if one tip finds sink, a pull on the brake that side may be needed to maintain the usual tension, followed by a dab on the other side to keep everything straight. This way you will find that you can keep on course easily; you will also be adding to your flight safety, because you will be helping to keep full pressure in the wing, which reduces the possibility of a tip tucking under.

If for any reason the wing tries to turn of its own accord — perhaps because of a tip deflation or a snagged line on launch — concentrate on keeping it flying straight by braking on the side away from the turn. Only when you are satisfied that you can keep it on a straight course should you even think about correcting the fault. A deflated tip on any but a high-performance glider will often correct itself without any input from the pilot. At most, a couple of long firm pumps on the brake should cure it — one is usually enough.

The left tip is deflated and hung up in the lines. The pilot is keeping things under control by braking the right wing to counter the drag of the deformed left one.

Ground speed and airspeed

Your paraglider *has* to keep moving through the air at a minimum speed of about 15 mph (24 kph) if it is to develop enough lift to fly safely. This is due to the laws of physics, and neither prayer nor large sums of money will alter it. Therefore in still air you will travel over the ground at the same speed as you fly: 15 mph (24 kph).

Now imagine that you are flying directly into a 10 mph (16 kph) wind: your airspeed remains unaltered at 15 mph (24 kph), but you will cover the ground at only 5 mph (8 kph), because of the headwind. This will feel quite slow, and even if you are close to the ground your speed will not seem at all threatening.

Things will feel rather different if you are flying *with* that 10 mph wind. You maintain your 15 mph airspeed, but now the 10 mph tailwind has to be added to it. You will be covering the ground at 25 mph (40 kph), which is quite likely to feel disturbingly rapid.

In all these examples the position of the brakes will be exactly the same, because the paraglider is passing through the air at the same speed. The big thing to remember is not to attempt to reduce your airspeed just because the ground is going under your boots more quickly than you might wish. **Maintain airspeed at all costs.**

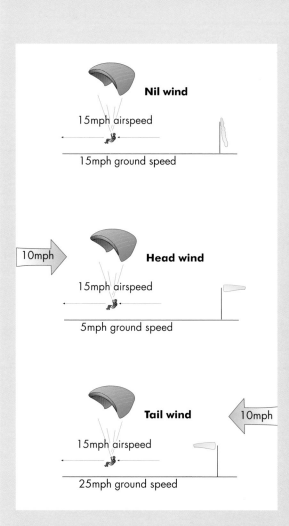

Figure 11: Never confuse airspeed with ground speed.

Turning a paraglider is so easy that you will find you are simply responding instinctively most of the time. Just a little pull on the right or left brake, and you are soon pointing in the right direction. When you have plenty of height and space to play with, that system works fine, but one day you will find that you are trying to stay up while ridge soaring in light conditions, with the ground only a few feet away: suddenly the precision of your turns will become extremely important to you. Under these conditions you need to turn as efficiently as possible without stalling or spinning. The secret is familiarity with your glider and lots of practice when the soaring is easy.

Yet another note of caution. Just because someone else on a similar glider is managing to stay up, don't assume that you can. You may not have the experience needed to turn safely near the ground. When it comes to handling, I sometimes think that a paraglider

Staying up on an old Air-Man XC 9, one of the first paragliders to be sold in Britain in any quantity. It will need only one sloppy turn to put Matthew below the ridge in these conditions.

Harness with cross-bracing. If the crossed straps in front of the pilot's waist are tightened up, side-to-side disturbance of the seat will be reduced when rough air is met during flight, but assisting a turn by weightshift will be difficult.

is much more like a horse than a motorcycle, and you have to develop 'feel'.

Weightshift

You can increase the rate of response when initiating a turn by using your body weight and leaning in the direction you want to go. Some gliders are much more sensitive to this than others — much depends on the spread of the risers and the design of the harness. On harnesses with adjustable cross-bracing, weightshift will only be really effective with the bracing slackened right off.

How much brake?

When dealing with turns, you will often hear pilots talking of percentages of brake. For practical purposes, zero brake is when the control handles are right up and the lines to the brakes have an obvious bow in each: the glider will be flying at full speed. The other extreme is 100 percent brake: the handles will be somewhere below waist height, and the wing very close to stalling. In between, at 25 percent brake your hands will probably be about level with your ears, while at 50 percent brake they will be at chest height. This is a very rough and inexact guide, but it won't be far out for most intermediate paragliders.

Speed and turns

The fastest turns are made starting from the zero-brake position. You pull one brake, say 25 percent or 30 percent, and round you go. However, this loads up the glider as you swing outwards due to centrifugal force, and your sink rate will increase considerably. So fast turns are not very tight ones and are greedy with height.

Tighter turns are achieved by entering with both brakes at about 25–30 percent and pulling the inside one further — perhaps as far as 50 percent. This produces a relatively slow, tight turn, which you can adjust by slight movements of the outside brake — always being smooth and taking care not to overdo it.

Whatever sort of turn you make, you will sink faster than when flying in a straight line, but the flatter the turn, the less the increase in sink rate.

At each end of the range of turns there is an extreme which you must be able to recognize and avoid. The extreme fast turn can develop into a spiral dive, while the extreme slow one is the start of a flat spin.

A *spiral dive* is entered by applying 50 percent (or more) brake on one side and keeping it there through a series of 360° turns. The speed and loads increase rapidly, accompanied by a dramatic increase in sink rate. After a couple of turns the speed really builds up. If you keep the brake on, the wing will bank more and more steeply as your body is thrown outwards by centrifugal force — eventually you can almost reach horizontal. During a severe spiral, you can become seriously disoriented and feel as if the world is turning around you. This is a good time to ease off on the brake — you should have done so much earlier. Unfortunately the disorientation effect can be so strong that pilots have been known to spiral completely airworthy paragliders into the ground.

The *flat spin* starts when you stall one half of the wing during a very slow turn. It is one of the most dangerous conditions you can get a paraglider into. As the name suggests, the wing attempts to rotate around its vertical axis with a strong yawing movement, and if left alone will do so, twisting all the lines together as it goes. Needless to say, the brake lines are included in this, so after a couple of full turns they are not going to be much help to you. Avoid the flat spin in the first place by not using excessive brake. If you sense that one may be starting, release both the brakes to get things straight again.

Your first turns will be gentle 'S' turns, and your instructor will gradually ask you to make these tighter as your flying progresses. He or she will be watching carefully to check that you don't make the common

beginners' mistake of forgetting to return the brakes to the cruising position after each element of the S. In the worst case, what might happen is something like this:

Facing page: *Changing direction — quite a lot of right brake is being used to turn this Barracuda.*

1 turn left using 25 percent left brake, and hold it there;

2 turn right using 50 percent right brake to overcome the left, and hold that too;

3 apply whatever left brake remains;

4 realize that the controls are now feeling sluggish, but still pull the right brake to try and straighten things up;

5 stall into the ground;

6 fill in accident report form.

Landing

Land into wind if you can. That's rule one, which means that your ground speed will be as low as possible. In fact it can easily be zero if there is any real headwind. We'll look at selection of landing fields later. For the time being, just imagine that you have a nice big green open space ahead of you with a windsock at one end and no other gliders in the air. Scan the area, make a smooth final turn at 40 or 50 feet (12–15 m), and line up along the line indicated by the windsock. Keep plenty of speed on by using very little brake, if any, and move your body into the fully upright position.

Full flare

If the wind is light, the ground will seem to be passing by very rapidly, but still keep speed on until your boots are about 3 feet (1 m) from the ground, then flare positively by using both brakes quite hard. If your co-ordination is good you will arrive with almost no forward motion at all, but always be prepared to run a few steps.

Wind gradient

The reason for keeping plenty of speed on during landing approaches is to counter the effect of the wind gradient. The wind speed close to the ground is normally less than higher up, because of friction between the air and the surface. The fast flight ensures that the paraglider keeps a safe margin of airspeed down through this wind gradient. Attempts at slow approaches can result in stalls because the wing may not be able to react quickly enough to a steep wind gradient.

The exception to the general rule about wind being lighter at ground level sometimes occurs among high mountains. Here valley winds can be blowing which are undetectable at altitude.

If there is a fresh breeze blowing, you will find that your descent will be almost vertical, and now your flare is much less important than the ability to collapse the canopy the instant you touch down. Often no flare will be needed, but I have seen pilots become so conditioned to flaring that they still do it the first few times they land in wind. Unfortunately, the landing is then followed immediately by falling over and being dragged backwards. As soon as you touch down in wind, turn and run towards the wing to deflate it, pulling in on the brakes at the same time.

The main sins to avoid on a modern paraglider are flying too slowly on the approach or trying to descend steeply in a series of stalls. The stalling descent used to be common in the old days of parascending canopies which were closely related to jump 'chutes, and those

pilots could get away with it, but it is a very risky business on anything else. You also need to make your final turn smoothly and with sufficient height that you don't arrive swinging about, penduluming from side to side.

Landings should always be light and easy, but if you have the slightest reason to think that everything is not going strictly according to plan, swallow your pride and prepare for a good PLF (see page 145) rather than trying to retrieve an impossible situation and ending up with a broken ankle. Certainly, if you are off-wind and making a crabbing landing, don't hesitate — go for the roll!

Of course, once you get further into the sport you will not always be landing in a field somewhere beneath take-off. You will be top-landing and slope-landing — techniques which are dealt with in Chapter 7.

Rules of the air

Launching, steering and landing are simple techniques to master on a paraglider, but they are just a small part of the overall blend of skills which will make you into a safe and confident pilot. The knowledge will come with time and a bit of study, but there are basic rules of the air which you need to know from the first time you venture into the air:

1 Aircraft flying towards each other — **break right**.

2 Aircraft on converging courses — **the aircraft on the right has priority**; the other one must change course.

3 Overtaking a slower aircraft while ridge soaring:

  – In the United Kingdom, **pass between the other aircraft and the ridge**.

  – In other countries, **pass on the outside**, taking care not to 'crowd' the slower aircraft.

4 On approach and landing — **the lower aircraft has priority**.

Where will I land?

When you start it is difficult to estimate where you will touch down. There is a simple trick which will help: choose a likely spot ahead of you and check whether it seems to be moving up or down in your field of vision. If it is apparently moving upwards, you will land short of it; if it is moving down, you will overshoot. This system is not infallible, because it assumes that you continue to fly at exactly the same speed and that the wind speed is consistent between you and the ground, but it is still a very good indicator which you can use from quite a long way away.

Facing page: Collapsing a stalled canopy at the point of touch-down in a fresh breeze

*Everyone joins in during the first
days at training school.*

Training schemes and pilot ratings

Most countries have a pilot rating system with several steps in it. The international standard is called Para-Pro which has been developed from a Norwegian hang-gliding system. Each step comprises flying tasks and examinations. The object of the exams is to equip you with the knowledge you will need to fly the next stage. Because paragliding is still evolving, the requirements tend to be changed from time to time.

The UK rating system

In the United Kingdom the rating system has four steps which cover all stages, from novice to advanced cross-country pilot.

The list that follows on pages 65–66 gives a general picture of the standards required for a self-launch pilot in Britain, where the hills are quite low and the emphasis tends to be on ridge-soaring in moderate winds. In alpine countries students tend to graduate to high flights much more early on, although in very light winds.

The requirements for tow-launched pilots differ in detail from those for self-launched pilots, but the overall progression is very similar.

Proficiency schemes and ratings

Although the Para-Pro system is available as an international standard, there are almost as many rating schemes as there are countries with paragliders in them. Many of these are adapted versions of existing national hang-glider schemes, but modifications are always needed. This is because, although it takes about the same amount of airtime overall to reach the level of competence at which you are little threat to yourself and others, the rate at which individual steps are attained is different. For example, most students get to grips with the basic technique of steering a paraglider within a few minutes, whereas it can take a couple of days to achieve similar precision on a hang glider. Conversely, ground-handling and launching a paraglider safely in a range of flyable conditions can take weeks to experience and master — it's rather more simple with a hang glider.

The philosophy behind a rating scheme can have a great effect on its usefulness. Some are biased too far towards experience, with levels being attained largely through hours of airtime and number of sites flown. That's OK as long as you appreciate that ten hours of smooth coastal soaring do not equate with ten hours of battling with mid-day thermals at alpine sites. Others depend too heavily on exam performances: pilots who are word-perfect in reciting the Quadrantal Rule for the Separation of Traffic in Controlled Airspace are still menaces in most paragliding situations if they haven't also learned the basic skill of keeping a good lookout when flying among their clubmates. From my own experience, I would say that the British scheme is fairly well sorted out, with perhaps just a shade too much emphasis on exams. As I write, there is a fine discussion going on in the USA about whether to change from a three-rung to a five-rung ladder. Time will tell, but as it will be the same pilots flying the same wings in the same conditions, provided that the selected scheme encourages the students to *think* as well as to fly, it probably won't make much difference whch is chosen.

We have to have ratings — governments and aviation authorities often demand it — and I would encourage anyone to keep aspiring to the next rung on the ladder. But always appreciate that reaching that rung does not by itself necessarily make you a better or a safer pilot.

1 **Student Pilot** This stage is completed while at training school. A dozen safe flights are needed, half of them with a ground clearance of at least 100 ft (30 m). The pilot must fly at appropriate speeds, make controlled 90° turns in both directions and perform a number of safe landings within a specified area. As well as these tasks, the student must satisfy the instructor that he can assess conditions, and devise and execute a suitable flight plan; and that he has a good attitude to airmanship and safety matters. The exam covers simple matters of flight and weather, as well as the all-important Rules of the Air (see page 61) for collision avoidance.

2 **Club Pilot** The pilot must demonstrate launches in nil-wind conditions and moderate breezes; must have at least twenty flights from a reasonable altitude — not 'ground skimming' — two of which must have at least five minutes above take-off level; and must execute accurate 180° turns and make good landings within a 20-m radius of a target, some of which must be top-landings. The exam requires more knowledge of air law and meteorology, as well as basic knowledge of the principles of flight. You also have to continue to convince the instructor that you have the sort of attitude and airmanship that will make you a safe pilot when you are in the company of others at club sites.

A mixture of students at club-pilot level and experienced members sharing the air on a pleasant soaring day

3 Pilot This standard prepares you for cross-country flying — if you wish. More stress is put on knowledge of air law and the principles of flight. Knowledge is required about stalls and spins, but you do not have to have to perform them. Much more flying is needed — 15 hours at the time of writing, and this has to be at a number of different sites. In both this and the next stage, airmanship and attitude continue to be taken into account.

4 Advanced Pilot This is the top rung of the BHPA training ladder. It is achieved by flying cross-country tasks as well as amassing a further 150 flights and 35 hours airtime. The knowledge required for the exam is quite extensive in all fields, and the successful Advanced Pilot will be qualified to a level comparable with that of the best recreational pilots in other branches of air sport.

During the Club Pilot stage an orange streamer about a metre long is flown from the pilot's harness until 10 flying hours have been logged. This is a signal to other fliers to allow extra space in the air, and it is also an invitation for club coaches or other experienced pilots to offer advice if it seems to be needed.

Attitude

Attitude is a recurrent theme in all the stages. Naturally, it covers attitude to personal safety and to flying itself, but it also goes much further. Paragliding depends on the goodwill of landowners, farmers and government agencies for access to its sites, and this must be carefully fostered. Leaving gates open, letting your dogs run about off the lead, and screaming at high speed through villages in cars plastered with paragliding stickers, are all examples of attitudes that the sport can do without.

The FAI Eagle proficiency badges require certain standards of achievement, and once attained do not have to be renewed. The requirements are the same worldwide:

Eagle badges

Badge	Distance	Duration	Gain of height
Eagle Bronze	15 km *and*	1 hour *and*	500 m
Eagle Silver	30 km *or*	5 hours *or*	1000 m
Eagle Gold	100 km *and*	5 hours *and*	2000 m
Eagle Diamond (Distance)	200 km	—	—
Eagle Diamond (Height)	—	—	3000 m

Holding an Eagle badge is not a qualification — simply a great source of personal satisfaction. The flights have to be observed by a responsible person, and a barograph is needed for the gain-of-height tasks. The badges are issued by the national aero club of the pilot's country, and a full register is kept. Often the national aero club will delegate responsibility for administering the badges to the appropriate national paragliding body.

IPPI card

It is easy for paraglider pilots to travel the world with their aircraft, but sometimes there are problems when proof of qualifications is required to fly certain sites or for access to cable-cars. The International Pilot Proficiency Identification card was introduced by CIVL in 1992 to overcome these problems. It carries the pilot's equivalent to the international Para-Pro rating in several languages. You still need your own national rating card — indeed, the IPPI is invalid without it — but there have been reports from all over the world that the system has made life much simpler for travelling pilots. The cards cost the equivalent of $10 in most countries, and in Great Britain they are issued by the BHPA. Get one before you travel abroad to fly!

The International Pilot Proficiency Identification card — very useful if you plan to fly abroad

Buying a glider and looking after it

When you were learning to fly, your training school will have provided you with gliders which were the correct size and which had a performance suited to your ability. Once you have qualified sufficiently to buy your own wing, there is plenty of scope for making expensive mistakes. Paragliding is a relatively new sport, and much of the knowledge which has led to the wing of the mid-nineties being remarkably safe has been earned at the expense of the customers of the late eighties.

There are second-hand paragliders on the market which are dangerous; there are those which are made from materials which were plagued by accelerated ageing, and there are plenty which are just downright old and obsolete. Unfortunately there are quite a few stolen ones too. Until you have built up a significant stock of experience, you won't be able to tell which is which, and it is a good idea to talk to as many thoroughly respected pilots as you can before parting with any cash.

In Britain the risks are minimized by purchasing from dealers registered by the BHPA, who will not sell uncertificated gliders.

Facing page: *The Windtech Ambar is a stable wing suitable for new pilots. Development during the 1990s has led to great increases in both safety and performance.*

A simple glider like this is perfect for your first few days of training, but its performance would be too limited for more ambitious use.

Certification systems

Don't let yourself become obsessed with performance alone: easy handling and stability are more important than the last degree of glide angle. As far as safety is concerned, you will encounter two main rating systems: *ACPULS* and *Gütesiegel*. ACPULS is principally French/Swiss, while Gütesiegel is German; both are recognized in many other countries. Both systems attempt to show how easily and how quickly paragliders recover from tucks, stalls, spins etc, and how much pilot input is required. However, the philosophy behind each is slightly different. ACPULS concentrates on how rapidly a canopy recovers from deformation, whereas Gütesiegel lays more stress on how easily it deforms in the first place.

The ACPULS system was revised early in 1994, and is now more correctly called AFNOR. Originally it covered twelve features of handling, from the simple 'inflate and launch' to flat spins and turn reversals. These have now been increased to seventeen, but not all gliders have to be tested for all the features. **Solo gliders** are put into one of three categories by the manufacturers — *standard*, *performance* and *competition* — and have to meet a different selection of the requirements, according to category. Naturally the standard gliders have to meet the largest number of requirements with the minimum amount of pilot input. **Dual** or **tandem gliders** make up a fourth category.

Dual gliders can have an area of 40 square metres.

The Gütesiegel (it means 'seal of approval') testing regime devised by the German hang-gliding association (DHV) is considered to be the more searching of the two systems. Gliders are graded from 1 to 3, according to ease of handling and recovery. A 'one' means that it will recover from a deflation almost before it has happened, while a 'three' will demand high-speed freestyle macramé with the rigging lines to stop the canopy turning inside-out in rough air. That may be a slight exaggeration, but you get the picture. Much committee work has been done to harmonize the certification systems, and it is very likely that a single system will emerge in due course

Figure 12: Examples of AFNOR **(left)** *and Gütesiegel* **(below)** *decals. These show that the wings to which they are applied satisfy certain standards of strength and handling. In future these, like the earlier ACPULS grading method, may give way to a standard CEN certification which will be identical throughout Europe. Never buy an uncertified glider of any type.*

The harness you use can affect the handling performance of the wing, and the airworthiness certificate
will specify the type that it was tested with.

Don't take anyone's word that any given paraglider
carries a certificate: make sure that you see it on the
wing itself.

Size is important

Your glider needs to be the right size for your weight.
Usually the wing area is indicated by a figure in the
model description, such as 'Space 26', which suggests
a nominal area of 26 square metres. At the time of
writing a 26 or 27 is a medium-size wing, catering for
pilot weights of between 65 and 85 kilograms. This is
clip-in weight, rather than get-out-of-the-bath weight.
Most manufacturers produce their models in three
sizes to cover the 45 to 120 kg range, plus a much
bigger one for dual flying and corn-fed Texans. The
airworthiness certificate which should always be
supplied with the glider will show a higher weight
range, because it refers to the all-up flying weight,
which includes the weight of the wing itself.

In smooth conditions you can get away with flying an
oversize wing, but as soon as the going gets rough you
will appreciate the wisdom of having one that is properly matched to your weight — lightly loaded wings
are much more prone to collapses. On the other hand,
if you are too heavy for the wing you are in for a miserable time, with difficult launches, a poor sink rate and
a fast landing speed.

Harnesses

The harness needs to be matched to the glider you fly,
although most modern designs can be flown with most
modern gliders. If you are buying a new one, you should
be guided by an instructor you trust. I would not recom-
mend any harness which does not include provision for
a back-protector and a reserve parachute with shoulder
connections. My personal taste is for adjustable cross-
bracing too. The cross-bracing dampens sideways

reactions in lumpy air. At the time of writing there is no international standard specifically for harnesses, although several countries have their own. In Europe, they may come under the umbrella of the European Personal Protective Equipment regulations in due course.

Common sense comes into harness purchase, and it is easy to try them for size and comfort by hanging from a rafter. Check that the leg straps don't feel as if they will cut into you, and select a model with a seat deep enough to support your thighs when you settle back into the flying position — some tend to be just too short. Avoid the so-called 'mountain' harnesses which have only a canvas seat and are uncomfortable after a very short time.

If buying second-hand, reject anything that is seriously scuffed, crudely repaired or obviously faded by extended exposure to the sun. Be prepared to spend enough for a harness you will be happy with for a long time, because you will probably change it far less often than the wing you fly it with.

John Silvester settling in after a high-wind launch. I like this kind of large harness with plenty of back support.

What paraglider should I buy?

You've been through the training school; you've enjoyed getting your Club Pilot rating; the sport is for you, so what do you buy? I would say: go for the latest model of a good intermediate glider (from the *performance* range of the new categories) from one of the larger manufacturers. This type will be pleasant to fly and the performance will not hold you back at all — they are well capable of cross-country flights. Buy a new one if you can possibly afford it, otherwise get a second-hand one from a reputable source. Avoid old-model 'hot ships' (pre-1992) like the plague, even if they appear to be very cheap and you are assured that they have only a few hours of airtime.

All paragliders depreciate in value rather fast, but the market for good intermediate gliders is strong, so if you decide you want to move on to a competition model in a year or so, you should be able to do so quite easily.

Rob won the World Championship on a Firebird Ninja in 1991, but many recreational pilots find it too demanding to fly.

One feature which I find really worthwhile is for the glider to have clear colour-coding for the lines. If the A, B and C lines are of different colours it makes life much easier when checking that they are all correctly laid out before launch. It also helps when there are tangles to unravel.

Everyday care

A perfect paraglider material would be completely impervious to air. It would also be cheap, light in weight, very flexible, reliably strong, not weakened by stitching or welds, totally tear-resistant, unstretchable, unaffected by ultraviolet light, and easy to attach lines to. Unfortunately such a perfect cloth has yet to be discovered, so for the time being the manufacturers all use woven materials of the nylon type which are then 'dressed' by applying various types of coating to ensure that they are not porous. This dressing is applied under pressure and heat, but it will not stay put for ever. The technology draws heavily upon experience of developing cloths for spinnakers on ocean-racing yachts.

The longer you can keep the dressing in your wing, the longer it will fly without performance loss. The dressing deteriorates very gradually, mainly owing to flexing and folding, but heat, mildew and sunlight all take a part too. You don't notice the difference as the ageing process develops, but it happens, sure enough. Just try comparing the crisp feel of the cloth of a new glider with one that is two or three years old.

You can slow down this ageing process with a little basic care:

- Don't fold the wing any more tightly than you have to: some pilots seem to develop a passion for getting it as small as possible. As long as you can get it in the bag, that's OK.

- Avoid rolling the wing up in a coil like a Swiss roll. This can build up considerable tensions in parts of the cloth. Instead, use folds with short flat sections between so that the cloth can relax between bends.

- If you are not going flying for a few days, try to keep your wing in a shaded space large enough for it to be taken out of its bag so that it is not under pressure.

- *Never* pack the glider away when wet. Let it dry out in the spare bedroom even if this poses a threat to household harmony.

- Try to lead the lines in smooth curves when you pack up. Avoid tight turns, particularly where they join the risers. This is especially important if your glider has Kevlar lines, as repeated bending can weaken them.

- Sunlight is bad news for paraglider cloth. When out of doors, keep it in the bag until you are ready to fly. This is particularly important if you are high on a mountain where the UV rays are relatively unscreened.

- Before starting out on a long journey, think about where you will put your paraglider in your car. Some luggage compartments have a hot exhaust pipe immediately underneath which is quite capable of baking it.

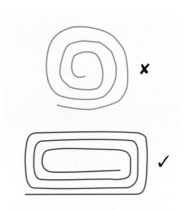

Figure 13: Folds are better than a tight coil when packing the wing.

Below: a well-folded wing

- If you really must clean parts of your wing, use a very mild soap and lukewarm water — *never* detergent or any other form of solvent.

- The public and paragliders do not mix well. Cigarettes, dog urine and sun-tan oil all pose a threat.

Increased porosity

A few years ago there was a problem with a certain type of polyester cloth which lost its coating very rapidly. After less than a year, new paragliders were becoming porous to the extent that they were difficult to inflate and could also stall in flight due to loss of internal pressure. Several different manufacturers in a number of countries used this cloth. Most of these aircraft have long since been withdrawn, and there is no chance of your purchasing one from a recognized dealer. However, be extremely cautious if you are tempted to respond to a newspaper advertisement, as there is a fair chance that you could be buying trouble.

There are instruments produced to measure the porosity of the cloth, and some paraglider dealers have these and offer a testing service. A crude check can be made by trying to suck air through a sample, but this needs lots of experience to be at all effective. You also have to pick the right place to check, because wings do not develop porosity evenly all over — usually the area behind the top of the leading edge is the first to go.

Karabiners and maillons

Karabiners and maillons are the essential links between wing and harness. Don't economize on them. Use either good-quality screw-locked alloy karabiners or stainless-steel maillons of at least 6 mm (¼ in) diameter. Karabiners are now produced which are specially designed for paragliding, being shaped to minimize any tendency to turn and thus avoid the load being taken on the gate.

Karabiners should be routinely replaced every three years, or sooner if scratched. They should be fitted so that the screw lock is in the inside — towards the pilot — as this reduces the tendency for them to turn just before take-off. Once in the air, always check that they have aligned themselves correctly.

If you need to loosen a maillon and are out on the hillside without a suitable spanner, you can often do the trick by gripping the nut between two coins to increase finger-leverage.

Rucksack

Most paragliders come complete with their own rucksack. If you are buying one separately, go for the large size regardless of the size of your wing. You will then have room for harness, flying suit and all the extras which can make a day on the hill so enjoyable.

Life will also be more pleasant if you have a broad Velcro strap to hold the canopy together when folded, and a thin nylon stuff-bag to keep it in.

Weather

Paragliding is a completely weather-dependent sport, so for enjoyment and safety you must build up some meteorological knowledge. This needs to be at three levels:

- a general concept of weather systems so that you can decide between going flying at the weekend or tiling the bathroom

- knowledge of how weather develops during the day in your locality, so that you can go to the best hill for the wind and recognize safe launch periods

- understanding of how air can move upwards powerfully enough for soaring flight to be possible.

In this chapter there is space only to scrape the surface of this vast subject, and I will use simplifications and generalizations which will make true meteorologists wince. For information on flying weather in detail, see Further Reading, page 196.

Weather — the basic ingredients

The air itself
The Earth is surrounded by air which remains there owing to the force of gravity. The air we are concerned with forms the *troposphere*, which is the lowest layer, extending from the surface of the Earth to about 40,000 ft (10 km) at its maximum height. *Tropo* comes from the Greek for 'turbulent', and the air here is always on the move. This layer is warmest close to the surface, and its temperature drops with height at a fairly constant rate.

Facing page: *A clutch of paragliders climbing in a blue thermal (see page 92)*

Air is a mixture of gases — mainly nitrogen, but about 20 percent is oxygen, and there is a small but highly significant amount of water vapour.

As we go about our daily lives at walking pace, it is sometimes difficult to imagine that air has mass, but stick your hand out of a car window at full speed, and the mass immediately becomes apparent. The gravity which keeps it in place around the planet causes the mass to exert considerable pressure, which can be measured with simple instruments; the most common of these is the barometer. Naturally, this pressure is greatest at the Earth's surface, because that is where there is the greatest depth of air to produce the pressure. Therefore, the higher you go, the lower the air pressure. If you take a barometer up a hill it will show this reduction, and when a barometer is used in this way, to measure vertical distance, it becomes in effect an *altimeter*.

Air reacts to pressure and heat in the way that all gases do: when it is heated its volume expands, and when it is compressed its temperature increases. Keep this in mind — uneven heating is the key to the generation of wind and lift.

The effect of the sun

If the Earth were not heated by the sun, or if it were to be heated completely evenly, the atmosphere would probably be prepared to remain as a sullen layer with little movement in it. As this is not the case, we will take a look at how the heating happens.

Because it is transparent, the sun's rays pass through clear air without heating it. When they strike the Earth, they are absorbed and heat up the ground or sea accordingly. You can experience this effect very easily by standing at a sunlit window on a winter day: you will feel the warmth of the sun on your skin, but if you place a hand against the window, the transparent glass will feel very cold.

The Earth's warmed surface radiates heat back into the air, which is thereby warmed from the ground upwards. This alone would be enough to cause considerable air movement, because as the ground-level air warms up it becomes less dense and will 'float' upwards, its place being taken by cooler air. This is how thermals develop, and we spend quite a bit of time dealing with them in the next chapter.

As there is lots of sunlight at the equator and not much at the poles, the overall effect is for air to rise at the equator and then flow towards the poles, sinking steadily as it does so. The rising air at the equator is constantly replaced by cold polar air travelling low over the hemispheres, and warming up progressively on the way. However, if this were the only influence, there would only ever be cold northerly winds in Europe, North America and Asia, and icy southerlies in Australia, South America and much of Africa. Variety is put into the global airflow in several ways:

- The planet revolves, so as one part is being heated, another is cooling.

- Land heats up much more quickly than water, and cools correspondingly quickly, thus adding to the unevenness of the heating.

- Not all the sunlight aimed at us gets here: clouds cause much of it to be reflected back out into space.

- The globe is spinning, and friction between the ground and the air layer next to it keeps it all going round more or less together. Of course, because air is fluid, there is plenty of scope for great variations, and complications set in when you imagine the conflict between the north/south/north (longitudinal) polar flows and the west/east (latitudinal) frictional effect. The result is a tendency for the air to move in vast eddies in which the winds obey some general rules (see page 82).

The Coriolis effect

We have Gustave-Gaspard Coriolis, a French civil engineer, to thank for this one. It is really difficult to explain without being able to wave my hands about. You can get a feel for it by looking at a long-playing record revolving on its turntable and imagining drawing a chalk line straight from the centre to the periphery. You would have moved your hand in a straight line, but the mark the chalk leaves would be curved because of the movement of the disc. The rotation of the Earth has a similar effect on the winds blowing over its surface, and this contributes to the tendency for air masses to rotate in moderately predictable ways. In the northern hemisphere the Coriolis force directs movement to the right; in the southern hemisphere it works to the left.

Lapse rates

As the pressure of rising air drops with height, it naturally expands and cools as a result. This is an *adiabatic* effect (that is, it happens without heat being transferred), and the rate of temperature loss with height gain is called an *adiabatic lapse rate*. The lapse rate varies according to whether the air is dry or contains condensed moisture (see Chapter 7). When the lapse rate is high, the air is often described as being unstable; conversely, stable conditions are said to exist when the lapse rate is low.

Clouds

Clouds consist of condensed water vapour in the form of minute droplets. At any given temperature, the air is capable of containing a certain amount of water vapour, which is quite invisible. When that critical amount is reached, the air is said to be *saturated*; beyond that point, the excess water vapour which the air cannot hold condenses into droplets and the moisture becomes visible. The temperature at which condensation occurs is called the *dew point*.

The warmer the air is, the larger the amount of moisture it can contain without condensation. Perhaps the simplest way of appreciating this is to look at the familiar effect of breathing out on a cold day: your breath, which has picked up moisture and warmth on its trip round your lungs, forms a small cloud when it meets the cold outside air again. Note that there is a gap between your lips and the 'cloud', because the air has to cool just a little before condensation takes place.

Back to real clouds and flying: rising air cools, and if it contains a significant amount of moisture, sooner or later it will cool enough for clouds to form. There are several types of cloud, and they are categorized according to type and the altitude at which they form. You don't need to know the details of all of them, but it is useful to be able to identify the main types and to appreciate the effect they will have on your flying day.

Cloud types

Cumulus clouds have a heaped-up appearance. At the lowest levels they are very obviously separate from one another, and even in the highest cumulus types (*cirrocumulus*) this separateness is still fairly obvious.

Cumulus clouds forming

Stratus clouds appear as sheets of cloud. These sheets can vary in depth from gauze-like *cirrostratus* to the thick depressing rain-laden *nimbostratus* of a British winter. You may also encounter *fractostratus*: these are the miserable little chunks which skulk about at low level under nimbostratus and are of no benefit whatever.

All *nimbus* clouds are associated with rain.

Cloud altitudes

The nature of clouds varies with the altitude at which they exist. They are grouped into high, medium and low clouds, but there can be a lot of overlap. There is also considerable variation in the heights of certain clouds according to the type of land beneath them — more of this later.

High clouds are the '*cirro*' group. These occur above 16,000 ft, and may be as high as 42,000 ft. The highest are the *cirrus*, which have the appearance of wind-blown wisps. These are sometimes called 'mares' tails'. Because the air at such altitude is extremely cold, clouds in the cirro group are largely formed of ice crystals.

Medium-height clouds are the '*alto*' group. Typically these are found between 7,000 ft and 20,000 ft. As well as the obviously-named *altostratus* and *altocumulus* types, *stratocumulus* lurks towards the bottom of the medium-height group.

Low-level clouds do not have a group name, but they are the ones with which you will become most familiar. *Cumulus* will be the ones you learn to recognize with most enthusiasm, because their fluffy cotton-wool presence marks thermal activity and the likelihood of good lift for soaring. However, it is quite possible to have too much of a good thing, and *cumulonimbus* clouds are the monsters of the whole cloud family. These are the thunderclouds. Their upward development is colossal: a strong cumulonimbus (usually shortened to *cu-nimb*) can reach from ground level to 40,000 ft or more. The energy associated with them is enormous, but it is far too violent to be of any use to paraglider pilots. The strong gust fronts in their vicinity can change the wind direction and multiply its speed in seconds. Avoid: cu-nimbs are life-threatening.

Rain

The minute droplets of condensed moisture which form clouds are so small that they have difficulty in escaping from the cloud mass — most remain within it, and those at the edges evaporate into the surrounding drier air very easily. However, they can eventually group together to build into much larger drops, and when that happens, rain is the result.

Air masses

When a large amount of air spends a long time in one place, it acquires the characteristics of the area. For example, air which passes slowly over North Africa can reasonably be expected to be warm and dry, whereas that approaching Europe from across the North Atlantic will be cool and damp; you can even think of great continent-sized cold slabs sliding slowly away from the polar regions. These air masses move, sometimes relatively quickly and sometimes very slowly indeed, owing to the global influences discussed earlier, but they are surprisingly reluctant to mix with each other.

Fronts

The margins between air masses are called fronts. These always involve a change in the weather and so are of great interest to paraglider pilots. The weather forecasts always give notice of approaching fronts, but their progress is also accompanied by characteristic cloud formations from which you can often gauge their positions for yourself.

Warm front

Warm air is less dense than cold air, so when a warm air mass moves against a cold one, its edge will tend

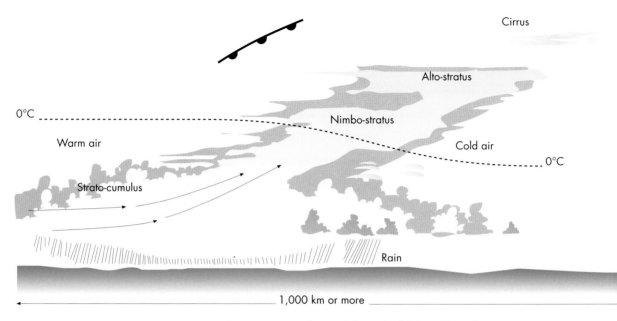

Cirrus

Alto-stratus

0°C

Nimbo-stratus

Warm air

Cold air

0°C

Strato-cumulus

Rain

1,000 km or more

Figure 14: Warm front advancing. This grossly simplified illustration shows the cloud types that characterize a warm front. Although we are used to seeing fronts represented by thin lines on a weather map, they are really quite broad areas of disturbance.

to rise up over the colder air. This effect forms a *warm front*. If the air which rises contains much water vapour, and it usually does, it will climb to an altitude at which the vapour condenses, forming clouds and rain. The length of the overlap will be several hundred kilometres, so the overall effect is quite gradual. The prime warning for the approach of a front is often a layer of cirrus across the sky.

After a warm front

While the front passes there will be heavy overcast conditions and rain, so soaring will be out of the question. Once the front is through, the weather will usually improve, but soaring conditions are rarely brilliant. The pattern of movement over northern Europe is such that the wind tends to settle in the west or southwest behind the front, and that means more damp Atlantic air.

On other continents the passage of fronts may not always be so noticeable, for a variety of reasons. For example, the effect of high mountain ranges such as the Rockies and the Andes can produce frontal effects at high levels which are barely recognizable on the

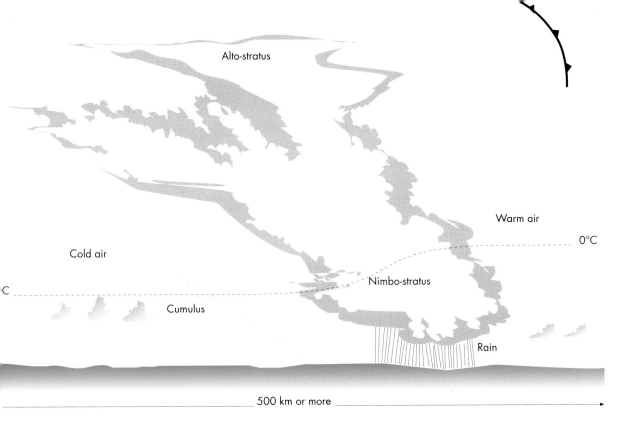

Alto-stratus

Warm air

0°C

Cold air

C

Nimbo-stratus

Cumulus

Rain

500 km or more

ground — although the weather maps will clearly show their existence. In the middle of large land masses the air will be generally dry, so the cloud markers that typify fronts in temperate maritime climates may well be absent.

Cold front

When a cold air mass is trying to overtake a warm one, its denser air pushes in under the warm air mass with a sort of blunt-chisel effect. This *cold front* lifts the warm air, which again tends to result in cloud and rain. The dense cold air moves the warmer stuff relatively easily, so cold fronts are steeper than warm ones and cover a shorter distance — even so it will probably be at least a hundred kilometres.

After a cold front

Not surprisingly, the air behind a cold front is relatively cool. In the northern hemisphere it also tends to flow from further north than is the case after a warm front, which means that it will also be drier. However, the sun is just as active in warming up the ground and the layer of air in contact with it. This is good news for the

Figure 15: Cold front advancing. Its width is far less than that of the warm front. From the ground, the altostratus clouds may conceal cumulonimbus too, if the front is particularly active. It is possible for a cold front to catch up with part of the warm front preceding it. The result is an occluded front, a sure sign that the associated depression is weakening.

soaring pilot, because the conditions for the formation of strong thermals are favourable. Remember, it is not heat alone which encourages thermal development, but the difference in temperature between the warmed patches and the air mass surrounding them, so after a cold front there will be scope for good temperature contrasts. After the passage of an active cold front, with its attendant rain and grim weather, the skies can clear surprisingly quickly, although the winds tend to remain on the strong side for paragliding.

If you are a beginner, the turbulent unstable conditions following the passage of a cold front may well be too rough for you, so check with an instructor or club coach before venturing into them. Don't imagine that because a few pilots are 'skying out', you will automatically enjoy trying to do the same.

Figure 16: The warm sector between a warm and a cold front. Note that the fronts near the centre of the low have become occluded.

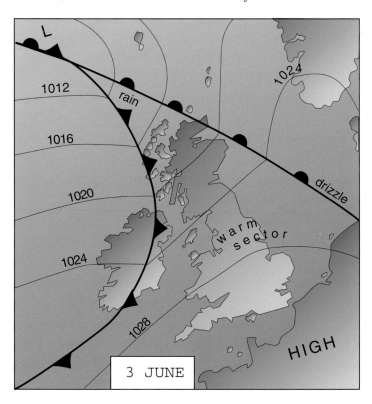

Sectors

You will often hear meteorologists refer to *sectors* — usually warm ones. You will see from the charts that fronts tend to radiate from the centre of weather systems. Sometimes they are widely separated, but often they are quite close together, in which case the wedge of air between the fronts is a sector.

Warm sectors are pretty disappointing, as they can feel like one long-drawn-out warm front, with lots of overcast and drizzle. Cold sectors are a lot more interesting, as they frequently mean that there will be a high lapse rate with the attendant strong thermal development (see Chapter 7, page 104).

Maybe we jumped ahead a little by examining fronts, because they are an intrinsic part of the weather systems which govern our soaring weather. In Britain and much of Europe, these systems are the depressions which follow each other across the Atlantic. The depressions are triggered by the activity of winds at great height — right at the limits of the troposphere — and they develop in a fairly regular and predictable manner. An initial small invasion of cold air into a warm mass is given a spin due to the rotation of the Earth, and the whole thing develops from there into an enormous vortex maybe a thousand miles across. Naturally, this spinning system soon incorporates its own sub-masses of warm and cold air, with their associated fronts.

As you try to make sense of weather maps and charts, you will become very familiar with the sight of the circular isobars surrounding a depression, and with the usually radiating lines of its fronts. Soon you will be able to judge the likely timing of various weather events associated with the system: really useful things such as whether it will be raining on Saturday or if the nearby hills will be blown out for the whole of next week.

Depressions and anticyclones

I cannot be alone in having difficulty in remembering which is which when it comes to anticyclones and depressions, so let's spend a minute or two getting used to them:

High-pressure area = high = anticyclone

Low-pressure area = low = depression

Note that lows are not referred to as *cyclones* at all unless they are of such a strength that they are developing into *tropical cyclones* or *hurricanes* (winds above 115 kph). In this case the paragliders will remain in their rucksacks, so you don't have to remember 'cyclone'.

Satellite view showing a depression centred on Scotland and its associated frontal systems

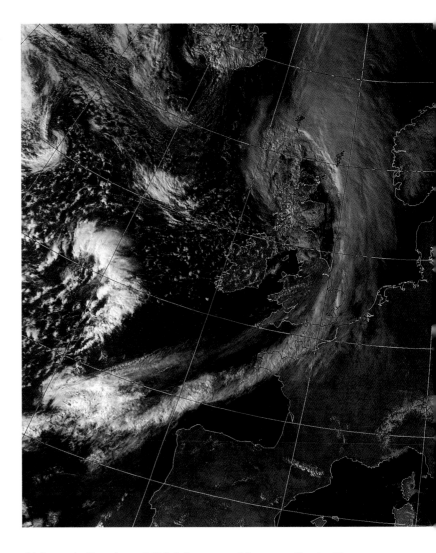

Although 'low' and 'high' as used here refer to the pressure of the atmosphere, if you were positioned out in space and if the air masses were visible, you would notice that they do indeed bulge higher over highs and sink lower over lows. I find that if I visualize an anti-cyclone as a heap of air, it is easy to remember; this may work for you too. This tip is very useful when trying to unravel some of the questions in the pilot exam papers.

Where is the low?
With a very small amount of practice you can indulge in some do-it-yourself forecasting simply by reading the weather map provided in the morning paper. From

the map it is easy to get a reasonable assessment of the probable wind direction and strength, but to apply this to the hills you are likely to fly it is useful if you can relate your position to the centre of the nearest low. Thanks to an observant Dutchman, there is an easy way: **if you stand with your back to the wind, the low will be on your left.** This law applies in the northern hemisphere only — if you are flying south of the equator, the opposite is true. The Dutchman was called Christoph Buys Ballot, and his name lives on in the form of Buys-Ballot's law.

Weather effects and soaring

All this information on weather systems and fronts allows you to judge the odds on the prospect of a fine day, but you need to know a bit more about how lift develops before you can hope to pick a good soaring day from a purely average one. The best ways of flying lift are covered in the next chapter, but here is how lift develops:

Thermals

We touched on this earlier: the ground does not heat up evenly when warmed by the sun, so consequently the air directly above it heats unevenly too. Air over a warm patch will eventually form a sort of bubble and move upwards powerfully enough to allow your paraglider to climb for as long as you can keep it in the rising air. There's more on this in Figure 22 on page 105.

The vertical progress of a thermal depends on its remaining warmer than the general mass of air, but as it climbs it cools, due to two influences: adiabatic cooling as a result of its expansion, and cooling through intermixing with the surrounding air. If there is moisture in the air, it will condense out to form a cumulus cloud when the thermal's temperature drops to the dew point. For the soaring pilot this is very useful, because the clouds mark the thermals. Also, with a bit of practice you can tell from the condition of the clouds whether the thermal is still active or if it is way beyond its sell-by date.

Cloudbase height

Example for a weather station at 1,000 ft:

surface temperature = 20°C

dew point = 15°C

Cloudbase height = 400 × (20 – 15) = 400 × 5 = 2,000 ft.

Add 1,000 ft for the weather-station height, to give a cloudbase above sea level of about 3,000 ft.

Cloudbase

Obviously, the higher the thermals are rising, the longer you will be able to climb in each one, so a high cloudbase is good news. Cloudbases vary considerably from country to country. In England, a mid-afternoon base of 6,000 ft is very good, while in the Owens Valley of the USA 16,000 ft is merely average.

There is a crude but handy formula for estimating the likely cloudbase: subtract the dew-point temperature from the surface temperature (in degrees Celsius) and multiply by 400. The answer will be the approximate height of the cloudbase in feet above the point at which the surface temperature was taken.

$$h = 400 \times (st - dp)$$

As there is a welcome tendency for hang-gliding and paragliding clubs to install small weather stations which give the temperatures this formula requires, it is worth remembering.

When there is little moisture present in the air, or when the thermals have cooled to the surrounding temperature below dew-point height, cumulus clouds will not form. Thermals unaccompanied by cloud formation are called 'dry' or 'blue' thermals (see photograph on page 78).

Wave

Wave is caused by the action of the air downwind of a ridge or range of mountains. As can easily be imagined, the airflow does not always immediately resume a placid laminar flow over the land behind a hill, but rather tends to settle down in a series of waves, each smaller than the previous one. However, there are circumstances in which one or more of these residual waves can become greatly amplified, so producing lift which extends to unexpected heights. If the windspeed is just right, second and third ranges of hills a few miles downwind can play a big part in magnifying the wave.

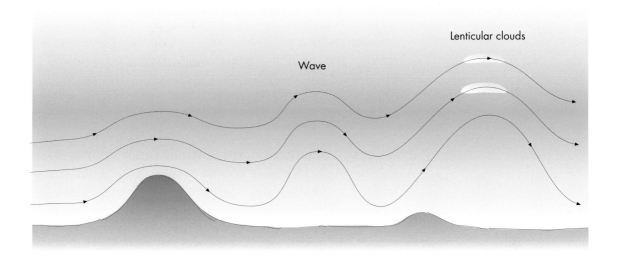

Lenticular clouds

Wave

Wave development is enhanced if there is a stable layer of air a short distance above ridge height, with unstable air above and below it. The unstable layers offer little resistance to the stable one, allowing it to oscillate much more than would occur if the air was either stable or unstable throughout. Specialized forecasting is required to predict such conditions, and their detailed consideration is beyond the scope of this book.

Figure 17: Waves develop downwind of a hill range in certain wind speeds and conditions. A second ridge can help to amplify the wave.

Wave is often indicated by long, narrow clouds with smooth boundaries. These form along the apex of the waves, much as a cap cloud does on a mountain. Because their cross-section is similar to that of a magnifying lens, these are called 'lenticular' clouds. They appear to be stationary in the sky.

It is interesting to note that only three or four years ago the idea of connecting with wave lift on a paraglider would have been considered impossible, yet performance — particularly top speed — has improved to the extent that (as I know from personal experience) it is occasionally possible to soar wave on some of my local Yorkshire hills. Don't get too ambitious, though: the air in the really big waves will be travelling at 40–50 mph (65–80 kph), which will be well beyond paraglider performance for some time yet.

Inversion

So far we have talked as if the air cools with height at constant and predictable rates throughout the troposphere. It does not — there are countless exceptions, but the simple inversion is one you will meet quite often: it consists of a layer of warm air on top of a cooler layer.

An inversion tends to form when the air is fairly stable, such as when a high-pressure system has existed for a few days; the cold air at altitude sinks very gradually, increasing in density and warming up adiabatically as it does so. Eventually a layer of air becomes established which is warmer than that immediately below it. Weak thermals will be unable to penetrate this layer, so vertical movement of air beneath it will be further inhibited. This situation can persist until the next front comes through and stirs everything up again.

Inversions are not good news for soaring pilots: the weather beneath them is often pleasantly warm, but the light will be hazy and the chances of good gliding conditions will be slight.

The air at a city site like this can easily become fume-filled during an inversion period.

Inversions are at their worst where a city is surrounded by a ring of mountains. The inversion can effectively put a lid on the whole area, trapping the city dwellers in with all their smoke, dust, pollution and humidity.

CHAPTER 6

Any meteorologist will admit that forecasting is not an exact science, especially in a group of offshore islands. Pilots in countries like Japan and Britain know this all too well. Generally speaking, conditions become more predictable as you go further into continental land-masses. Most of us watch the mid-evening TV presentations to get an overall idea of what the morrow may be like, but (in the UK, at least) they seem to be getting more and more vague. Many of the morning papers print reasonable synoptic charts which are useful and generally under-rated.

The following sections describe the main sources of more detailed weather forecasts in the United Kingdom; in other countries contact your governing body (see page 197) for advice on what services are available.

AIRMET

The Met. Office and the CAA jointly provide a selection of services for general aviation pilots, and some of these are very useful for us. AIRMET is the telephone version. You can get a detailed forecast which gives details of wind directions and strength at several heights, cloud cover, freezing level and much else. You may need some help in interpreting all the information at first, because it is given in 'av-met' jargon. Cloud cover, for example, is specified in *oktas* — each okta being one-eighth of the sky. The forecasts are updated three times each day and are obtained by phoning a premium-rate number. There are several numbers, according to the area for which you require the information. You can obtain a handy laminated card which gives the all these numbers direct from the Met. Office by phoning 08700 750075.

MetFAX

MetFAX is the fax version of AIRMET, but the range of services available is much greater. From any fax machine with a polling facility — most have that these days — you can obtain synoptic weather charts, satellite pictures and written AIRMET text. Like all

Weather-forecast sources

these premium-rate telephone services, it can become a bit expensive if you access it too often, but I rate the occasional forecast chart a good investment, particularly just before a weekend. Fax 09060 100490 (premium-rate) to receive the index page for all the MetFAX services.

Weathercall

This is another premium-rate phone service, operated by the BBC. Naturally it is much more general than those designed for aviators, but it has its uses. The United Kingdom is divided into twenty-seven regions, so the information can be quite specific. When the service was originally introduced I felt that they gave very little attention to predicting wind speeds, but that seems to have improved. Phone 09068 232 + your local area number — find out which your area is from your local BBC radio station.

Volmet

This is a weather-reporting service which is broadcast on Airband radio frequencies. It gives continuous reports from various airports of wind speed and direction, pressure, cloud cover, etc. Its relevance for powered aircraft is obvious, but for paragliding it is far less practical. Like so many things that are free, it somehow never turns out to be quite as useful as you had hoped.

The Internet

The Internet is a good source of weather information. The Met. Office has a Web service, MetWEB (http://www.met-office.gov.uk/MWIntro/MWIntro.html). There are also several free Web sites which carry detailed charts, and new ones appear regularly.

Wind and lift

When you are learning to paraglide you will be happiest in light, smooth wind conditions. Launching, steering and landing will keep you busy, and you will not mind landing at the bottom of the hill after each flight. However, before long you will be keen to stretch your airtime, and to do this you will have to seek out rising air and stay in it. You will have embarked upon the endless hunt for lift.

There are two main usable sources of lift for paragliders, and some minor ones as well. We look at the main ones first: *ridge lift* and *thermals*.

Ridge lift

A smooth wind of between 7 and 12 mph (12–20 kph) blowing against a steep ridge — say 2 km long and 50 metres high — is the recipe for unlimited airtime in your first season or two on a paraglider. The seaside is often ideal, provided that there is a continuous beach and that the cliffs are not completely vertical. The wind blows against the ridge and is deflected upwards in a broad band.

As long as you can remain in the parts of this *lift band* where the air is going upwards faster than the sink rate of your paraglider, you can soar. The band will be strongest just in front of the ridge, and reduces with height and distance out, as Figure 18 on page 98 shows.

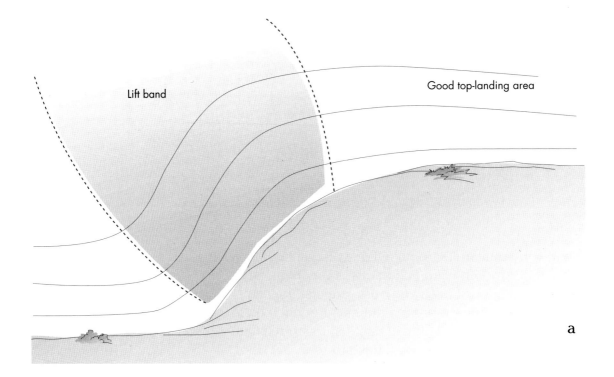

Lift band

Good top-landing area

a

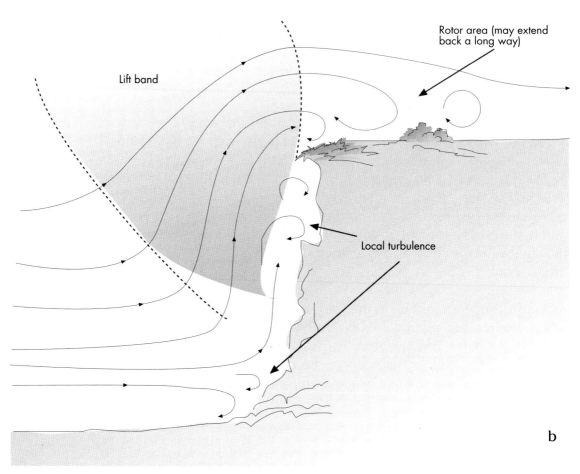

Lift band

Rotor area (may extend back a long way)

Local turbulence

b

There are several things you need to know about lift bands and ridges:

Figure 18 **(facing page):** *The airflow and lift bands over* **a** *a ridge, and* **b** *a cliff*

- They are at their best when the wind is at 90° to the slope, reducing greatly according to how far the wind is 'off'. No matter how easy the ridge soaring is, pay attention to the wind direction all the time. If the wind is even slightly off, you will find that you make faster progress in one direction than the other; keep monitoring this so that you don't suddenly find yourself down at one end of the site with no chance of making the return into-wind leg.

Preparing to soar a typical English moorland ridge

- More wind does not necessarily mean more usable lift; you may have to fly so fast to stay in the lift that you cannot exploit the minimum-sink performance of your glider.

- Air likes to change direction quite gradually. It greatly resents being required to follow sharp edges, and reacts by becoming turbulent. The edge of a cliff and the back of a steep ridge are places to avoid because the turbulence is extremely dangerous.

- Damp air which is forced to travel up a hill can condense and form a cap cloud above the top of it. The temperature only has to drop a small amount for this cloud to engulf the top of the hill, and soaring pilots with it. Watch out for this, particularly when flying during winter afternoons.

Figure 19: The route to take across the mouth of a gully is marked with a tick. Avoid the temptation to follow the contours and stray into the gully: it is all too easy to find that you are pinned there.

- When moving air is compressed, such as when wind enters a gully, it speeds up. You need to keep this in mind when crossing gaps in a ridge — you can easily find yourself unable to make forward progress if you let yourself become drawn too far back.

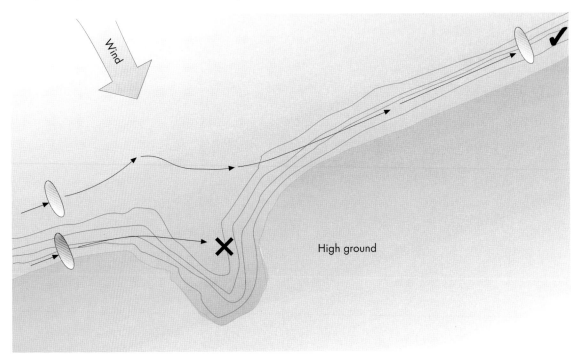

Wind

High ground

Wind gradient and low-level turbulence

At the levels reached by most paragliding activity, the wind speed increases with height. This is because the movement of the air closest to the ground is reduced by friction. It is very important to remember this if you are tempted to launch in wind speeds close to the top speed of your wing: you may discover that you are travelling backwards relative to the ground as soon as you have climbed a few hundred feet. On steep hills with valleys behind them this can lead you into very dangerous turbulence.

You also need to keep the wind gradient in mind when landing. This time it is the lack of wind speed which may bring the problems: you need to keep plenty of flying speed on to avoid possible stalls on approach. You must also expect your relative glide angle to flatten out as the ground approaches, so always make sure that you have plenty of field to spare.

Any obstructions on the ground will interfere with the airflow. Trees, houses, earthworks — anything can generate turbulence. The stronger the wind, the further the turbulence will extend. Watch out for the effect, especially when landing.

Figure 20: Turbulence generators

Top-landing

Soaring in ridge lift lets you build up lots of airtime, especially as you can usually land on top after an hour or so and then launch again after a rest. Top-landing has a certain mystique about it, but it is very easy indeed in soarable conditions. All that is required is to fly behind the lift band until you are in air which is flowing horizontally, and you will descend automatically. The main skill is in choosing the best route back over the edge of the hill. You want the way which will let you touch down directly into wind after making the minimum of turns. Naturally, if the wind is at an angle to the hill at all, you approach along the into-wind direction.

Gauge your speed over the ground very carefully during the last few feet. You will probably have to use very slight brake, and you should aim at landing with just a little forward speed. Be prepared to grab both back risers and heave down strongly to 'kill' the wing the second you touch down. Collapsing the wing with the B-risers is an alternative which some instructors now prefer; use the system which suits you and your particular wing.

Figure 21: Top-landing. The figure shows a ridge with a prominent spur. The wind is blowing many degrees off the hill, from the left. A and B show good approaches, with the gliders having to turn only a small amount to land directly into wind. C is much riskier, involving a fast approach while flying completely downwind, followed by a 180° turn into wind at the last minute. The area around D should be avoided in this wind direction: there will be sink and possibly rotor here, so don't be tempted to try to sneak across it to land right on the spur.

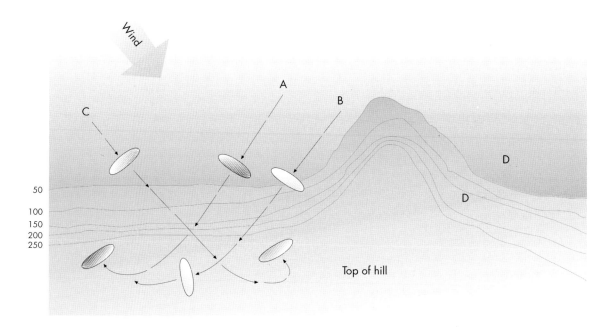

If you have judged wrongly and think you may go over the edge again, release the brakes, settle back into your harness and fly out with plenty of speed on. Never pile on the brakes in the hope of 'getting it in' — a stall in the rising air near the edge is a real possibility. This matter of going round again plays a part in your selection of a good top-landing spot. Always go for somewhere where the edge of the hill is smooth and where there are not lots of other fliers launching.

Slope-landing

This may be a good point to introduce the art of slope-landing. You will want to do this when the wind drops while you are ridge soaring and the alternative is a long flight down to the bottom — especially if your car is parked at the top. In essence a slope-landing is a carefully-timed low-level quarter-turn combined with a stall. Note that the order is important; vital even. Let's look at a typical sequence, paying attention to the decision-making throughout the procedure:

- Decide that there is not enough lift for a top-landing, so check out the slope for smooth areas free of rocks.

- If the wind is not coming directly up the slope, pay careful attention to its direction, and choose to land when flying the beat which is into wind. This will give you the lowest possible ground-speed on approach to touchdown, a very definite bonus.

- Refuse to be daunted by the proximity of the ground and the rate at which it passes by.

- Avoid being so gripped by the task in hand that you forget about other pilots who may be nearby. Keep looking around, as well as at your proposed landing spot.

- Keep flying at a good speed, so that there is no danger of stalling prematurely.

- At about 3 ft (1 m) from the ground, and sinking towards it, brake the outside wing firmly, and the moment the glider begins to turn away from the hill, stall it completely with both brakes to complete the touchdown. This is altogether a fast and fluid operation.

- Keep your options open if you can: if the area you first selected looks risky once you get there, be prepared to fly out and down rather than make a chancy landing.

- Beware of being half-hearted about the final stall. There is a real danger of finding yourself out of control, semi-stalled and flying out from the hill.

- Be prepared to make a PLF. Humans can't run sideways, so don't risk breaking an ankle trying to prove it.

- Collapse your wing fully at the earliest opportunity. Apart from the chance of its being blown away, a spread wing indicates 'I need assistance.'

Thermals

Chapter 6 gives the general idea of thermals (see page 91); here we look at them in more detail and try to work out how to find them and stay in them. By flying a paraglider, you are using the most sensitive form of aircraft to exploit thermal lift, but if you can't find it, that is not a lot of help.

Thermal formation

Before we get on to the interesting matter of using thermals to climb, we have to look further at the technicalities of their formation. The start is a patch of warm ground which heats the air directly above it. Because of friction and inertia, this air does not immediately float upwards, but remains in place for a time, with the bottom getting warmer and warmer. In this condition it is described as having a *superadiabatic* lapse rate. Eventually its buoyancy becomes irresistible,

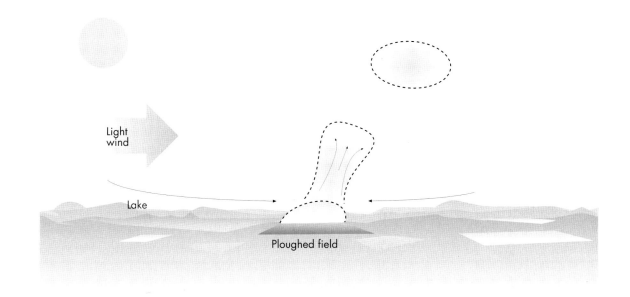

Light
wind

Lake

Ploughed field

and it breaks free and begins to float upwards. This it continues to do for as long as it is warmer than the surrounding air, which is cooling at the normal dry adiabatic lapse rate of about 3 C° per 1000 ft (1 C°/100 m). Naturally, cool air flows in to replace the upwardly mobile young thermal. If the patch on the ground is warm enough, this air may be around long enough to 'feed' the thermal further.

Of course, as it travels upwards, the thermal cools adiabatically, as well as through direct mixing with the surrounding air. Eventually, unless the air is extremely dry, it reaches a level at which it becomes saturated, and the condensing water vapour forms a cloud. This act of condensation releases heat (remember *latent heat* from school physics lessons?) which gives a final upwards push to the thermal. This explains why cumulus clouds have that heaped-up appearance. It also explains why lift continues into clouds, but does not provide an excuse for the dangerous practice of cloud flying.

The lapse rate of saturated air is only about half that of dry air.

First thermals
Your first thermals will find you, rather than the other way around. Typically, you will be having quite a

Figure 22: The development of a thermal — a stylized version!

smooth flight along a ridge or after release from a tow-line, when suddenly the wing will rustle quite loudly and you will feel a frisson of nervousness from the resultant turbulence. If you have a variometer and the presence of mind to listen to it, you will hear that 'climb' is clearly indicated. The air will feel more active then you have been used to, but you continue to fly straight, and after fifteen or twenty seconds there is another rustle followed by a surge of speed, and then everything is back to normal. You have flown straight into a thermal and then out of the other side. That surge you felt is typical of leaving the lift. Of course, more often than not you will just catch the edge of a thermal, when the feeling will simply be one of un-welcome turbulence, often coupled with a tendency for the glider to want to turn. This turning is caused by the part of the wing in the lift wanting to climb faster then the other one. This effect is very easy to feel on a hang glider, but I find it more elusive when under the much more flexible paraglider wing.

There are thermals of all shapes and sizes, and natur-ally their strength and height varies according to the air conditions and the time of day. For the purposes of illustrating ways of locating them and staying in them, imagine a 'standard' thermal which is originating over a dark ploughed field a little upwind of you. Think of it as being shaped like a giant wide-topped tower a hundred metres or so in diameter, and reaching from the ground to cloudbase. Now imagine it travelling along at about the speed of the wind, and sloping a little due to the effect of the wind gradient. In this simple thermal the lift is strongest up its centre — the *core* — and weakest at the edges. Your aim is to find the core and climb as far as possible in it.

Your vario is essential in this search. You should have used it enough to have become familiar with the notes it gives out for sink and lift without having to look at it all the time. Listen for a 'up' beep coupled with a rustle from the wing; if the paraglider feels as if it wants to turn you, resist the turn by turning against it.

Use weightshift as well as the brakes, and with any luck you will be rewarded with a continuous up-tone from the vario. You're in! Slow the glider a little and count to ten; if you are still going up, turn 180° back the way you came, counting to eight this time before S-turning back again. Keep S-turning, shortening the straight sections and controlling your speed so that you spend the longest possible time in the area where the vario tells you the lift is strongest. Amid all the excitement you must also make quite sure that no other aircraft are nearby.

Paragliders fly so slowly that it is quite possible to reach cloudbase by S-turn thermalling. This has the advantage that you are not likely to become disoriented or allow yourself to be taken downwind out of reach of your planned landing area. Until you are feeling really confident and have a constant awareness of others in the air, stick to it. Sooner or later, though, you will need to make 360° turns so that you spiral upwards (see **Turning in thermals** on page 108).

Finding your first few thermals will involve as much luck as judgement, but you will gradually develop a feel for it. Remember that between the thermals there is a lot of sinking air. You can use this to your advantage: on a thermic day: when the vario indicates more sink than usual, take this as a useful clue that there will be a thermal nearby. Let the brakes right off and fly as rapidly as possible through the sink, ready to slow down the second you find lift again. Deciding which way to go is really easy if you are soaring a ridge, as there are really only two choices of direction and your chances of guessing correctly are good. From a towline in flat areas the task is more difficult, and the best advice I can give at this stage is that if you did not sense any lift while on the tow up, your best chance is to search upwind. As your knowledge increases you will learn to identify local thermal generators such as silage stores covered with black plastic, or even dark areas of asphalt at runway junctions.

WIND AND LIFT   107

Don't expect all thermals to have a single core — or even an identifiable one at all. Just do the best you can to stay in the strongest part, and be grateful for every foot of free energy they give to your wings.

Turning in thermals

Although S-turning is quite a good way of thermalling, you need to master the more efficient technique of circling too. This is almost invariably referred to as 'three-sixtying' in gliding, as you turn through 360°. Anybody can make a paraglider do this, but the knack is to be able to turn at the speed which will let you make the best use of the lift.

I have asked a number of obviously successful pilots to describe their technique, and have learned enough from the answers to be satisfied that there is no single recipe. Suffice it to say that carefully judged differential use of the brakes is essential — just hauling down on the inside one is not the way! Also essential is to alter the rate of turn according to where the lift is strongest, so that you become truly centred in a core. Some pilots rate weightshifting as just as important as brake operation, especially for that initial turn into the thermal. In rough conditions this can introduce a dilemma, because if, like me, you enjoy the feeling of security given by tightening the cross-bracing on your harness in rowdy air, the weightshift response of your glider will be greatly reduced.

As usual, thermalling gets easier with every hour of practice and experience.

How fast should you fly when thermalling? There is no short answer to that except to warn against slowing down too much. You need to keep speed up to retain good inflation pressures in your wing so that it does not tend to collapse in the sometimes rough air of thermals. You also need speed to avoid spins when turning. It is easy to forget this when straining to keep the vario saying 'up', and allow yourself to slow down too much.

If there is any wind at all, the thermals will be taken along with it (unless they are so powerful that they overwhelm it — unusual in Britain, but common in some parts of the USA). Therefore, if you remain in one, you will almost certainly move downwind too. Unless you really do wish to embark on a cross-country trip, this means that you will have to make a decision to leave the thermal while still within range of your planned landing field. The ease with which you can move 'upwind' within the thermal will be much greater than in the air following behind it, so err on the side of caution at first. This is particularly important on ridges, when it is all too easy to go past the point of no return through paying too much attention to the vario. Normally this doesn't matter much — it just means a longish walk back to the edge — but if the ridge falls sharply away at the rear, there is a real danger of crashing in the lee turbulence.

Thermal markers

Although thermals themselves are invisible, anything being taken up in them will show clearly. The most obvious ones are other gliders, and birds. If someone nearby is climbing, simply fly across and join in, **remembering to circle in the same direction as any aircraft already in the thermal.** You will usually go up too, but sometimes you will arrive just too late and find only the sinking air beneath the base of a thermal which has completely separated from the ground and has taken the form of a bubble of rising air.

If you are soaring a long ridge on a paraglider and you spot gliders climbing fast at the other end, it is often fruitless to try and fly along to the same thermal. We glide so slowly that you usually arrive too late. It is often better to go in the opposite direction on the off-chance that a thermal will be developing there too. Many sites have 'house thermals' which occur at a particular point owing to the presence of a reliable thermal generator. With a bit of familiarity you get to know where they are, and will try these points frequently before casting further afield.

Strips of plastic being lifted by a vicious little dust-devil thermal at Chelan, Washington State

Gliders and birds are designed to fly, so their presence in thermals is not altogether remarkable. However, if the thermal is strong enough you can encounter items which were not originally designed to aviate. Pieces of chaff and straw are common at harvest time, and a large flying paper handkerchief suddenly spotted, uncomfortably close, from the corner of my eye once gave me a moment of disproportionate anxiety.

Before stubble-burning lost respectability, stubble fires were an excellent source of thermal lift for cross-country pilots, their plumes of smoke providing very positive markers. From my experience on hang gliders they were always extremely rough, and I suspect that they would be uncomfortably vicious on paragliders.

The most common indicator of all is in the sky — cumulus clouds which often mark the tops of thermals. However, from the ground these can be unreliable because you have to make allowances for the distance that they will be downwind of the thermal source, according to the wind speed. You also need to have built up some experience in judging whether they are the type which show the thermal is still active, or whether it is past its prime. Once you are a reasonable height in the air, it becomes much easier to make use of clouds as markers.

Not all markers are visual: if you are on the ground, wind speed and temperature can be a big help. I remember a spring day when a bunch of paraglider pilots managed to launch into sink time after time, while one or two others kept climbing out into good thermal lift. It was a light-wind day, and the unsuccessful fliers went off whenever the breeze felt strong enough to give ridge lift. The successful ones waited on the hillside through these bursts of activity, continued to sit it out through a few minutes of total calm, then launched at the next light stirrings — often into no more than three or four miles per hour (5–6 kph). The first group had failed to realize that the relatively strong wind — which felt all the stronger for being

noticeably cool — marked the *back* of a thermal which had just passed by. In contrast, the very light wind which followed a few minutes later really was a thermal, just there for the taking.

A little knowledge to store for the future concerns the way ground activity can trigger off a thermal. In the hilly districts where most of my flying is done this effect is rarely noticeable, but if you find yourself getting low over flatlands on a sunny light-wind day, you may be able to use it. Look out for a tractor harvesting, or a even a lone motorcyclist in a field, and adjust your track to pass overhead — many very low 'saves' have been made in this way.

Mountain thermals

So far I have written about lift which is generated directly from the wind or which is moved along by it,

Small cumulus indicate an active sky. You need to observe carefully to tell if the one you choose is developing or decaying.

because these are the usual conditions in my home-land, the British Isles. High-mountain thermals are different, however. The prevailing wind will necessarily be very light — the wind speeds that can be tolerated on relatively low, smooth hills produce fierce turbu-lence in mountains — so you will be relying on your skill at locating thermals if your flying is to be anything other than top-to-bottom every time.

Apart from the need for satisfactory lapse rates, the key to success is the position of the sun. As soon as the rays warm a slope, there is potential for thermals to form. All the normal rules apply — dark surfaces will absorb more heat than light ones, as will quarries and similar pockets which are out of any regular breeze. It follows that in the morning easterly-facing slopes will be more active, while in the afternoon the action will be on the westerly ones. In practice, it is usual to go to a convenient launch site and wait for convection to start. If the thermals are coming directly up the slope, that's fine; if not, you launch anyway and fly to a spur or face which is likely to generate action. A beguiling characteristic of alpine flying is that the choice of launch can often be dictated by the presence of a good approach road, a café at the top or just the com-pany of friends.

When faced with a glide down from at least a thousand metres, it is easy to be overwhelmed by the terrain and to fly about more or less at random, hoping to find some lift. Just a little imagination and flight planning can make a great difference to your airtime. Imagine that thermals usually travel up the faces of mountains rather than popping up at random in the valleys. They love to track up spines, and two small thermals will happily join together at the top of a ridge, continuing as one big one. Darren Arkwright, one of Britain's most successful hang-glider pilots, has a simple but graphic way of illustrating where thermals are likely to be in the mountains. He projects a slide — usually of the awe-inspiring mountains forming the Owens Valley in the western USA — and points out the planned flight route. Then he turns the slide upside-down and asks the audience to imagine that the land is a ceiling covered in condensation. At every point from which water would drip, there is quite likely to be a thermal.

Bear this in mind when you first visit the mountains. Instead of simply flying out over the valley to keep as much space under your boots as possible, plan your track so that it takes you along likely spines and over pinnacles. Then, when you find lift, fly it in just the same way as you would in lower terrain.

The lee-side thermal effect is at its best in mountains, too. This occurs when there is a wind blowing on one face and the sun shining on the other. Thermals form on the warm sheltered face. The problem is that you are quite likely to encounter rotor turbulence when you venture over the back to find them. In strong winds this can be very dangerous, but in light conditions the lee side can be a good thermal hunting-ground.

If you are going to fly in big mountains, you need to know and respect the föhn effect, which can produce dangerous wind effects that are not always obvious. The föhn is caused by an airstream being forced upwards as it travels over a mountain range. Cloud

Wind

Figure 23: Lee-side thermals are likely to originate in places like this.

forms and rain falls high in the mountains. Naturally the airstream is then much drier, and as it descends on the other side it also compresses and warms up adiabatically. Pilots who are tempted to fly in this apparently pleasantly warm airstream invariably emerge with horror-stories of turbulence and sink. The northern side of the European Alps is often subject to föhn conditions, and the Rockies are notorious for it.

While we are on the subject of mountain flying, here are some essential safety hints:

- Respect local knowledge. Always ask the local club or school about any special features of the site. Local dangers are not always obvious.

- If the locals are not flying, **find out why.** Blundering off in föhn conditions could ruin your holiday on day one.

- Don't let your search for thermals become so absorbing that you get into positions from which you cannot fly out and down to a safe landing.

- Carry a reserve parachute — one that has been repacked regularly and recently.

- Fly early in the morning and late in the afternoon until you are completely sure that you can handle the very strong thermals which you may encounter during the middle of the day.

- Remember that mountain weather can change extremely quickly. If there is any sign of cumulo-nimbus clouds developing nearby, land and pack up quickly.

- Valley winds can switch in seconds, so use any wind indicators you can find before finally committing yourself to the landing direction. Smoke, flags and clothes on washing-lines are all useful if there is no windsock to be seen.

Convergence

In the lift context, *convergence* is the name given to the condition existing when a moving airflow meets an opposing one and the air is forced upwards. In one form it happens when two or more thermals flowing up separate sides of a mountain join together at the top or spine. The resultant area of lift often appears much bigger and smoother than you would expect from the sum of the contributing thermals. Another form, and a very common one, is when a sea breeze meets a light prevailing wind from the land. This frequently produces a convergence line, marked by a chain or band of clouds. It is sometimes possible to fly into the convergence and track along it for considerable distances. A favourite place for this is the area south of the Sussex Downs in southern England, where hang-glider pilots such as John Pendry and Johnny Carr pioneered long cross-country distances in sea-breeze convergence. Later Michel Carnet and Rob Whittall made some of the first long British paraglider flights in similar conditions.

Towards the end of writing this book I encountered quite a dramatic form of convergence. Chelan Butte is a small mountain which stands at the apex of a 'V' formed by the valleys of the Columbia River and Lake Chelan, in Washington State. I launched from the Butte one evening, expecting maybe some ridge soaring, but was surprised to climb without effort for over 2,000 ft. The area of lift covered several square miles, and I could fly over the lake and town at will. The effect was convergence caused by the meeting of airflows following both valleys, and is apparently well known in the area. It didn't last for more than an hour, and hang-glider pilots launching later found no more than the expected ridge lift.

Magic lift and wonder wind

Some hill and mountain sites are famous for providing a very pleasant form of lift in the evening. The usual effect is of smooth and uniform lift which is reliable but not particularly strong. It starts late in the evening, fading away as darkness approaches, and can be so beguiling that it is easy to soar on in the fading light at hilltop height only to find that the landing field in the valley bottom is in almost total darkness. There are two main sources of this lift:

- **Trees** If the valley is heavily wooded, especially with broad-leafed trees, they soak up heat all day while the sun is high, to release it later as the ambient air temperature drops in the evening. This can provide gentle lift over very large areas. It is sometimes called the 'accumulator effect' or 'magic lift'.

- **Katabatic flow** down an eastern-facing slope which boosts the anabatic flow up the western side of a valley. The sun sets in the west, so eastern-facing slopes go into shadow long before western-facing ones. Naturally the air on the eastern side then cools and tends to 'slide' down into the valley. This gives an extra push to the western-side air, which is already doing quite nicely because of the sun and the angle of the slope. The result is smooth lift which extends further than would be expected for such a light breeze. Not surprisingly, the name 'wonder wind' is sometimes used for this.

Smooth soaring on the wonder wind, with Ingleborough hill in the background

It can be fashionable to underrate these types of lift because they do not lead to great cross-country flights. I think this is a pity, and I hope you will make the most of them whenever you get the chance. Apart from the beauty of the scene, it also gives a great opportunity to get your harness perfectly adjusted and to tune your speed system.

Wave

The mysterious way in which wave lift develops has been covered in Chapter 6 (see page 92). Paragliders do not yet fly fast enough to be able to exploit major wave systems, but you may experience milder forms of the effect, so you need to understand it and to be able to make the best of it when you connect.

If you do enter wave, it will probably be on a hill site with some similar ridges upwind. The ones I'm familiar with are those in Wales and the north of Britain. You will launch into ridge lift, which will feel normal for about 300–450 ft (100–150 m). Then there will be a brief period of moderate turbulence, followed by smooth lift which may extend up for thousands of feet. At first you will think that you have found a particularly benign thermal, but after a short while it will occur to you that there is no need to turn at all — simply parking into wind is enough to keep the vario chirping, apparently indefinitely.

A couple of thousand feet gained like this can feel very high indeed; somehow the smoothness makes you feel more exposed than does the hurly-burly of thermalling. Keep checking your progress: you will probably find that you are stationary relative to the ground, and you should ease the brakes off enough to edge forward if possible. If all is well, try tracking up and down the area of wave lift, which may extend far beyond the limits of the hill you launched from — remember, it originated a couple of ridges upwind of where you are flying. If your experience is like mine, you will just be beginning to feel at home with the height when all of a sudden the vario starts saying 'down only' and you are back at ridge height within a few minutes. The wave has switched off by going out of phase.

A flight such as this depends on the wave being in exactly the right position. The problem is that it will shift quite a lot with only a slight change in overall windspeed. The situation can arise where another pilot notices how well you are doing, launches to join you, and immediately experiences frighteningly rough air which sends him to the bottom of the hill in a few seconds. This will be because the wave has moved upwind enough to put the launch point into its lee downdraught. I have seen this effect make a normal top-landing area into an aluminium scrapyard as a succession of hang gliders discovered that 'wave' and 'lift' were not always the same thing.

Occasionally, particularly in winter, you may find that in a sky that is otherwise completely overcast with stratocumulus there is a long narrow patch of clear sky just parallel with the front of your ridge. This will be a 'wave slot', and you may be able to fly up through it so that you are eventually looking down onto the sunlit tops of the clouds stretching away into the distance — a brilliant contrast to the grey day you took off in. I've not managed this on a paraglider yet, but I achieved it once or twice on relatively primitive hang gliders which didn't have much performance.

There are risks to playing this game, the main one being that the wave may change slightly and close the slot with great rapidity. On such a slow aircraft as a paraglider you will not be able to dive through a closing slot, and may easily find yourself in a danger-ous and illegal position, out of sight of the ground.

It is easy to become over-concerned with the technicalities of lift. Theory is no substitute for getting into
the air and searching for the wonderful sources of free
energy that are there for the taking. Provided you have
enough knowledge to recognize potentially dangerous
conditions such as föhn, cumulonimbus cloud development, and encroaching hill fog, the best way to
refine your knowledge about lift is to fly it. There is
immense exhilaration and satisfaction to be gained
just from making the most of the day and getting to the
'top of the stack'. And getting high and remaining there
is also the key to the next big step in the adventure
that is paragliding: flying off across country … We look
at this in Chapter 11.

Practice

*Approaching the landing field at
Annecy as a threatening storm
brews in the mountains behind*

Advanced equipment

The instruments which paraglider pilots carry with them are virtually identical to those which have been developed in the other soaring sports — hang gliding and sailplane flying. This is a field which has developed greatly during the past few years, and if you can afford it, you can strap a bewildering selection of electronic equipment to your harness. However, don't be dismayed if your budget is limited, because you can become a good pilot without buying an array of elaborate instruments: a simple variometer and a basic altimeter are all that you really need. Nowadays these are usually combined into one unit.

Variometers

The variometer, or *vario* as you will normally call it, indicates the rate at which you are climbing or sinking. When you are starting to fly paragliders, the prospect of ever getting so far above the ground that you need something to tell you whether it is getting nearer or further away may seem unlikely, but you will soon find that it is very hard to tell — even from as low as 200 ft (60 m).

Varios work by sensing the change in pressure of the air around them. In the most basic form this is done by using a flask with a couple of interconnected transparent tubes communicating with the outside air (see Figure 24). Two very lightweight loose plugs, generally referred to as pellets, are in the tubes, which are slightly tapered. Imagine you are on the ground: the air pressure is steady and the pellets sit at the bottom of their tubes. When the flask is moved up into less-

Instruments

Facing page: *A fully equipped competition pilot. The vario/altimeter is on his right, and will swing into position as the risers go taut. His map has slipped down his leg and will need to be retrieved once the flight is under way.*

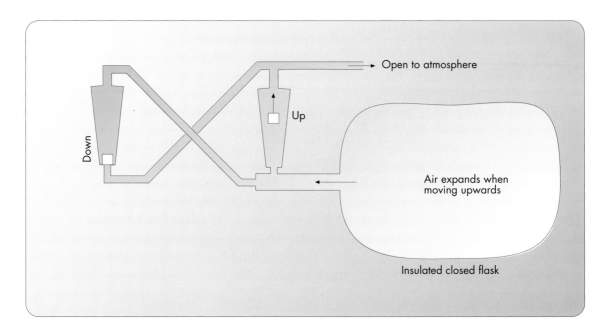

Figure 24: A simple pellet variometer. The taper in the tubes is greatly exaggerated.

dense air, some of the air in it flows out, raising the *up* pellet up its tube as it flows. Once the pressure in the flask equals that of the outside air, both pellets sit at the bottom of the tubes again, but as soon as the instrument moves down into denser air, the flow will be into the flask: now the *down* pellet will be lifted until the pressures are again matched.

These simple instruments are now virtually obsolete, although some of the Makkiki brand, manufactured in Hawaii, are still around. For paragliding, this type of vario is not ideal because they are inevitably bulky, must be upright to operate correctly, and are entirely visual — no audible tone is possible. However, they have the benefit of not requiring batteries, so I have noticed one or two competition pilots carrying them as backup instruments.

For many years the mainstay of lightweight vario design was the *thermistor* type. These again used a flask, but instead of moving pellets, two small heating elements were placed in the tube. According to the flow of air, one of these would be warmer than the other, and this differential was measured and indicated electronically. These varios were sensitive and effective, and many are still in use. Thermistor varios usually have a sound-generator wired into their circuits so that climb or sink is accompanied by an audible tone as well as the movement of a needle. Indeed, on some of the most basic models, a tone was all you got. This type of vario works well, but is more fragile than the *pressure-chip* models (see below).

Paragliding has developed almost hand in hand with pressure-chip varios. As the name suggests, these use a tiny pressure-sensitive cell integrated with chip circuitry. Much of the technology of this was originally developed for fuel-management systems in vehicles, and our sport has benefited from the large amounts of research money that has been spent in this field.

These varios are now extremely sensitive and versatile. They can respond to vertical changes of only a few centimetres, and can be programmed to give their information in a variety of ways. These include average rate of climb or descent rather than constant reading, and total-energy readings, which require the forward airspeed to be measured as well as vertical speed; and naturally there are all sorts of options concerning the type of sound signals. As mentioned earlier, altimeters are routinely included, and a thermometer function is common. Flight information can be stored within the instrument, to be printed out later, and an accurate clock can be included. In effect, what was once a simple device has tended to become a compact computer which tells you what is happening while you are flying and stores the information for later inspection if you wish. In its most developed form, the vario has become a barograph too (see page 130).

The software within these varios has opened up possibilities which would have sounded like pure science-fiction not long ago, notably the speed-to-fly feature. Briefly, this indicates the most efficient speed to fly to maximize glide in given lift conditions. To be effective, the vario needs to have stored information about the glider's performance — you will encounter this as its *polar curve* graph (see page 26). This you may not have conveniently to hand; never mind, the vario can be used to generate the polar and store it for future use. What's more, you can keep the information for your own access alone by means of the built-in password security system which acts as a form of thief-deterrent.

An ingenious feature on at least one model is the ability to arrange the display on the screen in the form that is most suited to your use. For example, for paragliding you may want the screen to sit on your leg in 'portrait' format, whereas a hang-glider pilot may prefer the wider 'landscape' arrangement on the bottom bar. The instrument lets you choose and then arranges all the 'dials' and digits accordingly. Luxury indeed.

It is easy to be so impressed by all this technology that you feel you have to buy the latest and most fully-featured instrument, but until you have been soaring for a season or two you will probably be more at home with a relatively simple vario/altimeter. Here is what I would be looking for as a first-time buyer in the UK:

- a display which you can read easily in bright sunlight — some of the early LCD screens were a bit dim;

- an analogue (dial-type) display for the vario;

- a digital display for the altimeter, reading in feet;

- altimeter readily switchable between QFE and QNH settings (see pages 190 and 192);

- ability to have the tone on up only, or on up and down;

- a strong case without any sticking-out bits;

- ideally, the ability to switch to a spare battery during flight.

- I am prejudiced against models which require you to press buttons in combination to switch between functions. This is because when under pressure — such as when piloting a paraglider with other aircraft around me, or in any but the smoothest air — I know that I am entirely capable of forgetting what the combinations are. You may not suffer from such a handicap.

All that will narrow the field considerably.

Buying variometers
If at all possible, try before you buy — there really is no substitute for an hour in the air with the instrument you are thinking of owning. Most dealers will let you do this, but if it is not possible, or if you are buying secondhand, then try the following tests:

- Have a really good look at the instrument, inside and out. If there is corrosion around the battery terminals or signs of home-made repairs, reject it at this stage.

- Read the instruction booklet. If there isn't one, you may like to wonder why. Unfortunately varios are sometimes stolen — usually minus booklet.

- Switch on the unit and check that everything that should be able to be set to zero can be set to zero.

- Are any switches that you may need to operate in-flight too dainty for use with gloves on?

- Raise and lower the unit slowly a few times, at arm's length. Check the zeros again, and then take it up a flight of stairs and note how it responds. Will you be able to hear the tone with your helmet on, or alternatively is it so strident that you would cheerfully stifle it? Is it over-damped or under-damped? Is there a significant lag in its readings? Is it over-sensitive, so that it squeaks every time you look at it? Now take it back to where you started from, and check that everything is back at zero without having to be re-adjusted.

- If the instrument is a multi-function one, repeat the operation for all the functions — referring to the instruction booklet to make sure that you understand them all and haven't missed any.

The scale on the vario can be in feet per minute or metres per second — it isn't really important which. However, altimeter readings are most useful in feet, as these are the units of elevation used on air-navigation charts.

It's well worth getting instruments you will be really happy with. They are important. You will probably use them for years, and they will be with you for every minute you are in the air.

Airspeed indicators

Because of the relatively small overall speed range of the aircraft, airspeed indicators (ASIs) are of limited use on paragliders, although for serious cross-country thermal flying they can be worthwhile. And let's admit it, it is sometimes fun to get an idea of how fast or slow you can travel. However, a really good reason to have one is for checking windspeeds at launch.

There are three main types: *disc*, *venturi* and *turbine*.

The cheapest ASIs are the popular Ventimeter and Hall disc instruments. These consist of a transparent tapered tube with a guide wire up the middle, an air inlet at the base, and an outlet at the top. A plastic disc is free to slide up the wire, and is happy to do so when the inlet is held into wind. The speed is read directly by checking the disc against gradations marked on the tube. The Dwyer meter uses the same principle, but with a little plastic ball moving up the tube. All these instruments have to be aligned with the wind to give accurate readings, but if this is done they give excellent results in spite of their simplicity.

Venturi ASIs use a vacuum gauge to measure the depression in a venturi. The higher the speed, the greater the depression. The Winter meter is the best known of this type, but they are little used in paragliding. As with the disc models, the venturi must be accurately aligned if reliable readings are to be gained.

Now to my favourite: the turbine. In these a small fan rotates a tiny magnet. The revs are counted electronically and translated into airspeed displayed digitally on a small LCD screen. I keep one of these in the pocket of my flying suit, and use it frequently. The turbine will tolerate a few degrees of misalignment without giving erratic results.

Turbine ASIs can be incorporated into varios, with the turbine sensor unit being mounted on the outside of the case or at some remote point and connected by wires. The remote-mounting option allows it to be fitted to a part of the aircraft where the airflow is least influenced by the wing or other obstructions such as you, the pilot. I have seen them lowered below the harness, attached to a long lead, and with a vane to keep the sampling head in line with the airstream.

Compass

Like the airspeed indicator, a compass will not be necessary until you start to attempt ambitious cross-country thermal flying, although one can be quite handy when checking wind direction on the ground at unfamiliar sites.

There are two uses for a compass: to follow the correct bearing when trying to cover miles across country, and to keep you flying straight when in cloud. As cloud flying is at best marginally legal as well as being really stupid, I will mention the cross-country use only.

Briefly, you need a fairly large spherical compass which is effectively damped. The best place to mount this is on the chest strap of your harness, making sure that it will not be influenced by any other instruments or by the radio, if you are using one. Compasses tend to be useful only on long straight glides. The constant turning when thermalling confuses magnetic compasses, and even the best ones can take a long time to settle down again after you have stopped circling.

GPS

GPS = Global Positioning by Satellite. This would have sounded like a science-fiction dream when I started flying hang gliders, yet now neat little units are available which will tell you at a glance where you are on the surface of the Earth, accurate to 50 metres or so. If you are above the surface of the Earth, they will even tell you how far above, although it must be said that they are not always quite so accurate at doing that.

GPS instruments operate by constantly monitoring their position relative to a number of satellites which are in geostationary orbit 11,000 miles above the Earth's surface. The accuracy is amazing, even though it is understood that the information accessible to private pilots is deliberately degraded in comparison with that which military pilots can receive. For the average club pilot a GPS system is an entertaining novelty, but serious cross-country pilots really gain benefit. Nick Przbylski in South Africa was one of the first people to apply GPS use to paragliding, and when Rob Whittall went after world records there in 1993 he found it invaluable. Using GPS and radio on the glider and in the retrieve vehicle not only ensured that he was flying the right track, it also enabled Nick to have the car standing by at touchdown after several hours of flight over rather featureless country.

Giving your position is only one of the facilities that GPS offers. Probably the most useful feature is the ability to programme into the instrument a series of points along a proposed route (waypoints) from take-off to goal. Then, as you fly, the GPS gives constant progress reports indicating the bearing to fly, your average speed and the estimated time of arrival at the next point. You could have chosen the waypoints to ensure

Full instrumentation. This package is on a hang glider, but it could equally easily be used on a paraglider. The GPS is on the left; the central unit contains a variometer, digital altimeter and ASI (the chromed cylinder is the ASI sensor); on the right is a remote-control unit for a video camera mounted on the keel.

that you keep clear of controlled airspace — always a matter of anxiety for cross-country fliers — or to find turnpoints on a competition flight. If you are at the start of a paragliding career you may find it hard to imagine the need for such assistance, but as soon as you embark on cross-country flying the benefits will soon become obvious.

GPS is here to stay, and I guess that there will be a tendency for map-reading navigation skills to disappear during the next generation or so. However, they are still essential for the time being, because GPS is not completely reliable and there can be blind spots from time to time. There is some way to go before GPS does for map-reading what the pocket calculator did to the slide rule.

Barographs

We touched briefly on these under the variometer heading. They are instruments which produce a permanent record of the flight, usually in graph format, showing the altitudes reached against the duration. It is very satisfying to see the evidence of a good flight, and if you intend to register a flight as an official record, a barograph reading (barogram) is essential.

Early barographs used a stylus marking on a revolving drum to produce the flight record, but now the state-of-the-art instruments store the information electronically and deliver a print-out when the flight is over. If you are going to the expense of buying a barograph and have any record aims at all, make sure that it is a model approved by CIVL for records.

Instrument mounting

Most instruments are so small and light that they can be mounted in a variety of ways. The most common is a Velcro strap around wrist or thigh, or attached to harness straps. As all the best manuals say, experiment with different positions until you find the one you prefer. I have settled for the vario on my right thigh. If your flying suit doesn't have a loop or two to stop the strap from slipping, it is worth stitching at least one on. The alternative is to pull the strap so tight that your lower limb goes to sleep, or to discover the vario round your ankle during the critical phase of a tricky launch.

No matter how little you value your instruments, always use a mounting backup in the form of a strong cord. Dropping anything except fine sand or water ballast from a paraglider is dangerous and illegal. It is also inevitably expensive.

Whether it is called a reserve, a backup or a rescue system, we are talking of a secondary parachute to get you down safely if your main paraglider stops flying properly for any reason. There are many on the market, most of which operate in the same basic way. They draw on almost twenty years of steady development in the hang-gliding world. The principle is simple: the pilot pulls a handle which releases the still-packed parachute from its container attached to the harness, in a little parcel. The parcel is then thrown into clear air, where it opens as soon as it has fully extended the bridle which connects it to the pilot's harness. The canopy and lines have been carefully packed into the parcel in such a way that they develop in sequence, rapidly and without tangling. The parcel-wrapper is called a deployment bag.

The most common type uses a small canopy which is connected to the harness via its lines and a bridle shaped like an inverted V. The apex of the bridle connects to the lines, the legs joining to the harness at maillons fitted just behind the shoulders. Some older types use just a single point of harness connection, and others are connected in front of the shoulders. I am unable to work up any enthusiasm for these older solutions. All the types described so far are completely unsteerable.

Several manufacturers are now introducing steerable reserves. Most of these are round canopies with slots in the back which provide some forward speed, or delta-shaped like Dr Rogallo's very first kite designs — a case of the wheel turning full circle! These steerable models use two risers, each of which terminates near a shoulder. They are steered by pulling on the appropriate riser. The response is much less positive than steering a paraglider, but they do give you the chance of facing into wind for the landing.

Finally, there is also at least one rectangular ram-air design which has a very good glide performance but requires that you 'cut away' from the main canopy before it deploys. A single pull on the deployment handle initiates both the cutting away and the deployment. The concept is elegant, but I would need a lot of convincing that it would not require more height in which to work than the more orthodox types. Also, it depends on the departing main canopy to pull out the reserve — not much comfort if you are already tangled in the main …

No matter what sort of reserve you have, if you ever have to use it in anger, a PLF (see page 145) should be an essential feature of your arrival, as the descent will be steep and probably fast.

It is important that any reserve you have is short enough to deploy underneath your paraglider wing. In the early days, reserves were used with bridles connected via long strops, hopefully to get the reserve well clear of a semi-flying main wing. This is the system used for hang gliders, but it is not so good for us because of the risk of entanglement. The short reserve system has turned out to be the most dependable.

Most reserves are manufactured in at least two sizes, and you need one which suits your weight. There is usually an overlap in the pilot-weight ranges which the canopies can handle, and if in doubt my preference would be to go for the larger size. These may take a fraction of a second longer to open, but the descent rate will be significantly less.

You will see the expression 'pulled apex' in descriptions of reserves. In these types an additional line runs from the bridle straight to the apex of the canopy and pulls the centre down towards the pilot. This speeds up the opening time and slows the descent rate compared with a domed canopy of the same diameter, but at the expense of less stability on the ride down.

You may come across rocket-deployed reserves. These originate in the USA, and they use a small but very powerful rocket to draw the 'chute out. They may be effective, but frankly I am not at all happy about their use by the average sport paraglider pilot. I am assured that an accidental deployment is virtually impossible. However, having seen the hang-glider version demonstrated on the ground, even the remote chance of one firing on one of our typically crowded European sites seems distinctly unappealing. Especially if I should happen to be in line with it.

Your reserve 'chute will be no good if it stays in its container when you really need it. It must work first time, every time, yet never appear uninvited. Think of it as a system, all parts of which must work perfectly together. Nowadays most harnesses include provision for reserve mounting, but if you are using one from a different manufacturer, check very carefully that its design is compatible in every respect. This is not a job for the amateur: consult an expert — preferably a qualified rigger.

Reserves need to be repacked regularly. This is a job you can do for yourself provided you have the correct handbook, follow it religiously and understand the deployment principle perfectly. Many clubs run packing evenings supervised by experts, and these are the best places to start.

Reserve canopy use and care

- Familiarize yourself with your system. Hang your harness up somewhere — in the garage, maybe — and practice grabbing the handle until you are confident that you would find it every time in a real emergency.

- Repack often and carefully.

- Don't attempt to repack on your own without the correct handbook for the canopy.

- Take just as much care of your reserve as you do of your paraglider: keep it dry and away from heat and solvents.

- When replacing elastic bands used in repacking, never use stronger ones than were originally supplied.

- Take extra care when packing pulled-apex canopies. These usually require the use of a length of cord as a rigging aid during packing, but it is absolutely vital that the cord is removed at the right time during the process, or the canopy will not open.

- If you are tempted to inflate your reserve on the ground to see what it looks like, prepare to be surprised at just how hard it pulls even in a wind of three or four mph.

- Remember that the reserve is a *system*, every part of which must be kept in perfect condition. There have been several recorded cases — at least one fatal — of the handle coming adrift from the deployment bag when pulled hard, because of old or inadequate stitching.

Drinking water

A good container for liquid can be a vital part of your equipment, particularly if you will be flying in a hot part of the world. The drinking systems made originally for mountain bikers, which consist of a flexible bag and a valved-mouth tube, are often adapted for paragliding. 'Camelbak' is one popular make, and some harnesses are now produced with special compartments to take the system.

Ballast

Competition pilots often carry ballast in the form of water, usually in a pillow-shaped bag under the seat. The additional weight (10 kg or more) makes the paraglider easier to handle in the strong thermals of the middle of the day, and can be discarded later in the flight to allow the pilot to make the most of weaker lift as the day calms down. If you are planning a competition career, look out for a harness with a compartment to take a ballast bag. For normal recreational flying such an extra is quite unnecessary.

Liquid supply

Japanese world-record holder Masahiro Minegishi carrying glider and ballast to launch near Kitakyūshū

Above: *Helmet choice is still a matter of personal preference.*

Right: *1993 World Champion Hans Bollinger (Switzerland) models a stylish pair of Oakley shades.*

Doing it all safely

As I said in the Introduction, there is some danger in paragliding. The choice of how much danger is really up to you. With a sensible approach the risk is very small indeed, but if you tackle the sport at all recklessly you will certainly pay for it — possibly with your neck. Although I am going to offer you my own ideas of safety — ideas built up from over twenty years of hang gliding and paragliding as well as those shamelessly stolen from whoever thought of them first — don't imagine for a minute that this is all there is to the subject. Make this *your* chapter too, by adding your own elements of safety and sharing them through your club or association.

I separate the aspects of safety into three: *passive*, *defensive* and *active*. Your overall safety depends on a constant interaction of all three categories. It also depends on remembering Murphy's Law, the constant companion of any aviator: *If anything can go wrong, sooner or later it will*. And there's more: *it will go wrong at the moment when it can cause the biggest trouble*.

Don't go it alone

I believe very strongly that safety in the air depends greatly upon building your own sense of responsibility and self-reliance, and I hope that this book will help you in this. However, I must stress again that the guidance of qualified instructors and coaches is one of the greatest aids to safety in the sport.

Passive safety

Pay attention to all the elements of passive safety described below: they are essential to your overall safety habit.

Flying equipment

Safety starts with your equipment. Don't compromise on anything. Fly a glider that is the correct size for your weight, and use a comfortable harness that is easy to get into, with a good back protector and a professionally fitted reserve parachute.

Helmet

The choice of helmet is a problem. At present there is no published standard for helmets suitable for air sports, so either we have to use those developed for other activities, such as cycling or motorcycling, or we go for so-called 'paragliding' helmets which are often simply one man's idea of what he thinks would do the job and sell well. He is not always right. Take these points into consideration and then buy a helmet that you feel is right for *you*.

- Look for good protection of the temples: many cycling helmets are poor in this respect.

- A tough outer shell is useless if there is not *plenty* of the right types of padding between it and you. A close-fitting Kevlar shell may make you look like a hero of the skies, but some such models seem to offer little protection against brain damage, compared with less glamorous types.

- A helmet is only any good if it stays in place. The design of retaining strap plays a bigger part in helmet safety than you might imagine. This is an area where a helmet which complies with standards for other uses is likely to score over an unmarked one.

- A helmet is only any good if it fits. Try lots until you are really happy with your choice.

- Make your own decision about which type of helmet to go for: 'open', 'full-face' or 'chin-protector'. Face protection is obviously a good thing if you find yourself being dragged over rocky ground, but may be less of a blessing if the unthinkable happens and you need mouth-to-mouth resuscitation. I am also rather uneasy about the way some guards extend a considerable way beyond the chin: they look to me as if they could exert an undesirable twisting load in some types of accident.

- Some people don't mind flying with their ears covered. I'm not one of them. I prefer to be able to sense
  my airspeed by the sound of the wind, and don't like
  to wear anything which may add to my isolation or
  even prevent me from exchanging shouts with other
  fliers.

Sunglasses

With any luck you will spend quite a lot of time high
up in the air with little shade. You need sunglasses
which give good UV protection at the very least. For
eye-safety it is also desirable to filter out the infrared
wavelengths, but this is less widely publicized. You will
find that lenses that filter the blue part of visible light
increase your perception of cloud; this is not strictly a
safety feature, but it can help you to locate thermals by
spotting the birth of little cumulus clouds.

Naturally, choose shatterproof lenses, and if the glass-
es are at all a loose fit, use one of those elastic retain-
ers which fit onto the ends of the ear-pieces. Some
pilots use skiing goggles for winter flying, and these
can incorporate all the foregoing features.

Gloves

I put gloves very high on my list of essential equipment
for passive safety. I virtually never fly without them,
regardless of temperature. Obviously the thickness
depends on the season, and I like skiing gloves in
winter and thin leather ones in summer. The point
about wearing them all the time is that paragliding can
damage your hands in two ways at least. One common
source of wounds is skin burns from the lines. The
canopy only has to get mildly out of control in a fresh
breeze while you are holding a line rather than a riser,
and you can get burned to the bone in no time. I have
also known pilots to get quite nasty finger burns when
pulling the lines to form 'big ears' (see page 155). The
other common injury occurs when being dragged by a
canopy. If you are desperately reaching around trying to
pull the thing to a standstill, you will be very glad of
gloves. And yes, it can happen to you …

If your flight is likely to last for more than a few minutes in cold weather, you will also discover that paragliding is second only to motorcycling for numbing the fingers. Quite apart from the inescapable fact that the temperature decreases as you climb, your hands are exposed to the wind for every moment of the flight, and will spend much of the time up above your shoulders — thus making it relatively hard for the blood to be pumped around them.

On the subject of skiing gloves, it is worth removing the snap hooks which the manufacturers supply to clip them together in pairs. Nobody ever uses these hooks, which are probably simply there to ensure that you lose two gloves instead of one, so cut them off before they catch onto a line when you are doing an alpine take-off. This is not an imaginary fear: I have seen it happen.

Hand injuries, even if only to the skin, are so disabling and slow to repair that you should do all you can to avoid them. As soon as you are away from the controlled environment of a training school in summer, use gloves all the time you fly.

Boots

Boots give protection and grip, and you should never paraglide without them. The market is now big enough for one or two sporting-equipment companies such as Salomon to make special paragliding boots. These offer good cushioning and ankle protection, as well as having a weatherproof flap to conceal the laces. Ideal. However, many other types of boot will do, provided they are high enough to cover the ankle and have soles with clearly defined grips. Avoid boots with hooks for the laces, as these are fated to hook around a brake line during ground-handling or tangle with the speed system when in the air.

Good boots may seem like a luxury when you are starting paragliding, but you will soon find that you will spend quite a lot of your leisure time wearing them, so don't over-economize.

Spinal protection

The science of back protection for paraglider pilots is still in its infancy, so you will have to rely on your own common sense to help you decide what to choose. Back protectors produced for other sports seem to have limitations when applied to ours. In particular, motorcycling ones do not seem to me to extend far enough under the buttocks. My feeling is that virtually anything is better than nothing, but it is a good idea to clarify the idea of what a spinal protector needs to do before you make your choice.

Keep in mind that in paragliding your bottom frequently arrives at the accident before the rest of you. In the very early days this may be because of a misplaced desire to 'stretch the glide' by keeping your feet up so long that you land sitting down. Later, when trying to soar a small ridge in scratchy conditions, a little local turbulence may be enough to dump you onto the ground before you have time to get your undercarriage down. Injuries due to seated landings range from the extremely painful broken coccyx through to permanently disabling damage further up the spine, or even brain damage through vertically transmitted shock.

In any of these cases a semi-rigid protector which extends from under your seat to midway up your back may lessen injury, but — like the crash helmet — it needs a good thickness of shock-dissipating foam between you and it.

Some protectors are designed to deform progressively on impact, while others are extremely stiff. The stiff ones must also have some padding if they are to be effective.

You need to look at back protection in conjunction with your harness: obviously, one must fit the other. Also, beware of stiff protectors which come too far up your back: there must be no risk of the top of the back protector chopping into the base of your skull in a crash.

Back protector by Air Bulle. This is a serious attempt to provide a progressively deformable protector, and it looks as if it would be effective.

One particularly novel form of back protection is available with the Apco Paradise harness. This consists, in effect, of an inflatable armchair which is activated by pulling a toggle on the harness, or whenever the emergency parachute is deployed. I guess that this does not strictly conform with my idea of passive protection, and my personal choice is for something which really is there all the time.

Other equipment

Carry a whistle and a webbing cutter in your flying-suit pocket or somewhere you will be able to reach them even if you are disabled. Don't tuck them into the back of your harness.

If there is any chance of ending up in water — perhaps when practising radical manoeuvres or soaring sea cliffs — a buoyancy aid is essential. There is a popular idea that air will be trapped in a paraglider wing in the event of a water landing, so no lifejacket is necessary. Air *may* be trapped, but that will be no use at all if you are beneath the wing, sodden through, and tangled in some lines. You need a buoyancy aid which will keep *you* upright with your head out of the water. Never mind the paraglider!

Defensive safety

Under the heading of defensive safety, I include all those things you can do to minimize damage or injury by just looking ahead a little. By developing good defensive safety you can outwit Murphy and his law. To a large extent, defensive flying is a state of mind which can be cultivated. Observation is a big part of it.

Defensive safety includes matters of natural caution, such as avoiding flying a new glider and a new site at the same time. It also covers details like moving your launch point a few metres one way or the other if it means that there will no longer be a barbed-wire fence downwind of you — even if the fence is so far back that you don't think there is any real chance of your being dragged back onto it if you get the launch wrong.

On a larger scale, it means never committing yourself to a single plan. Always have a second and third option ready to slot into position the moment it is apparent that Plan A is doomed to failure. For example, when you set up a top-landing, ensure that there is a clear path ahead of you in case you find you need to overfly and go round again. And if the lift then dies, you should already have a clear idea of where your bottom landing will be. Always keep the words of Mark Dale, the BHPA's Technical Officer, ringing in your ears: 'Never put yourself in a situation where it's Plan A or disaster!'

Here is a list of items which come under my heading of defensive safety. I hope that you will be able to add to the list throughout your flying career. The big trick is to add the items through foresight rather than bitter experience.

- Pre-flight checking. Not just the canopy and lines etc, but also the pins on your back-up parachute **before each launch.**

- Pre-flight planning. Know the limits of airspace around your proposed flying site. If it is one likely to be affected by military low-level flying, phone the relevant warning number at the earliest opportunity (see page 193).

- Weather awareness. Don't fly without some idea of what the weather is likely to do, and keep watching throughout the day.

- Don't fly alone, and make sure somebody knows where you are going and approximately when you are likely to return.

- Until you are very experienced, carry a wind-meter, and respect your own limits for air speed at launch.

- Be prepared to walk to a safe launch-point rather than using the close but dodgy one.

- Similarly, rate safety higher than nearness to your car when landing.

- Make taking care of your equipment an automatic everyday part of your flying routines.

- Don't let your wing languish for hours in the sun.

- Repack your reserve parachute frequently.

- Keep current. Flying and judgement skills soon get rusty. Ease your way back into the air with a few unambitious flights if you have had to take a break for any reason.

Defensive safety is one step ahead of passive safety, but sometimes the two categories overlap. Suppose, for example, that you decide to take some in-flight photos using a bulky SLR camera. Would you hang it round your neck so it rests on your chest the way you do when using it on the ground, or is there a safer way? If you think of the camera as your own personal rock which you might easily fall onto, rather than as an expensive instrument, you may decide that it would be a better arrangement to hang it to one side, at about waist level.

Active safety

Under this heading I include all the actions and reactions which will either keep you out of danger or minimize the effect if things go wrong.

Figure 25: The parachute landing fall. The full sequence could make the difference between life and death in a crash after a big deflation. It involves using the bent legs as shock-absorbers at initial touchdown, and then smoothly rolling down one side of the body and across the back. Most untidy paraglider arrivals under a fully inflated canopy do not require the entire sequence, but stages 1–4 will save leg, arm and spine injury time after time.

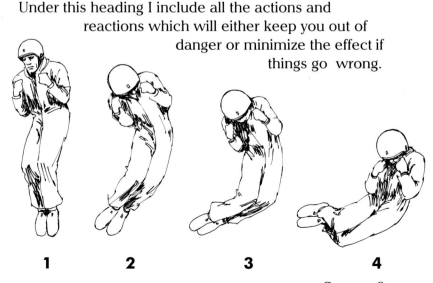

1　　**2**　　**3**　　**4**

Top of the list is keeping a look-out all the time you are in the air. Know where the other pilots are. Remember that mid-air collisions are potentially fatal, and don't imagine that they only happen in the most crowded conditions. In fact, when it is really crowded, everyone tends to take more care — the really nasty mid-airs tend to happen when there is quite a lot of space around but pilots are concentrating on thermalling rather than keeping a constant look-out.

The parachute landing fall (PLF)

The PLF is a vital active safety technique to master. As the name suggests, it was developed by military parachutists as a way of reducing injuries caused to heavily-equipped men descending fast on unsteerable canopies. The overall idea is to spread the shock of landing progressively over all those parts of the body that can best absorb it, while protecting the parts which are easily damaged.

The basic technique is to make the first land contact with your feet tightly together and knees slightly bent. Then follow through by spreading the load over the side of the legs, the buttocks and diagonally across the back as you collapse and part-roll to a halt. You fall in the direction dictated by the approach, never attempting to resist.

Throughout this procedure the hands are kept knuckles-together in front of your chest with your elbows tightly against your sides. Your chin must be tucked in and your back rounded. One of the hardest parts to master is the knack of not being tense: your body should be as

Stages in the PLF:

1 Ready to meet the ground: legs firmly together, knees bent, no tension in knees or ankles

2 Contact: legs together, flex at knees, chin and elbows in. Make no attempt to anticipate the landing by pushing with the feet.

3 & 4 Collapse progressively onto thigh and hip.

5 Keeping elbows and chin well in, roll across back.

6 & 7 Come to rest as the energy is expended. Check that all parts are working, and be thankful you practised PLFs earlier.

5   **6**   **7**

relaxed as possible, while at the same time you need to make a conscious effort to keep feet and knees tightly together. At no time must you reach out with hand or foot to try to arrest the landing.

All the descriptions in the world are no substitute for a little practice at PLFs. Your instructor should introduce you to their delights quite early on, so that you can slip into PLF mode automatically whenever the time comes. Because paragliding in Britain draws from the military-influenced parascending/parachuting back-ground, the PLF seems to be taught very well here, but I know that schools in some other countries almost ignore it.

Hang-glider pilots converting to paragliders find it quite difficult to do PLFs, because they are so conditioned to making running landings that it feels natural to hit the ground with the feet in the ready-to-run position. That's OK for a completely controlled arrival on a flat surface, but if the slightest element of crisis seems to be creep-ing into the event, the PLF is by far the safest option. Occasions to decide on a PLF in good time are when landing cross-wind or while travelling backwards.

One of the problems with PLFs occurs in high wind, and demands rapid action the moment you are down. If you have retained the brake handles (you should), and have bunched your hands against your chest in the approved manner, you will discover that you are maintaining the canopy in the perfect configuration for a high-speed drag across the ground. Be ready to haul in one of the brake lines immediately.

Cultivate the habit of standing up immediately after every successful PLF, so that anyone watching will realize that you are unhurt, and then gather in the wing as soon as possible. A paraglider open on the ground is universally accepted as a sign for 'assistance needed'.

It is quite natural to want to help your friends in their flying, but you do have to do this thoughtfully and carefully. Sooner or later you will be tempted to assist someone making a launch in a high wind. You probably had some help like this at your training school, so it won't seem too unfamiliar, but don't just blunder in without a thought. There are at least a couple of ways your well-meaning help can lead to big trouble. Imagine this scene:

It is blowing about 20 mph (about 30 kph) on the edge of a hill, and a pilot you don't know particularly well has managed to get his wing inflated but is being gradually moved backwards while on tiptoe. You rush forward, grab his harness and start to pull him forwards. Unfortunately, the convenient point you selected to pull on was his reserve 'chute handle. You remain holding this while the pilot departs smartly backwards.

Now imagine almost the same scene, but this time the pilot is hovering at shoulder height, going neither forwards nor backwards. Trying to be helpful, you approach from behind and grab hold of the pilot's seat at each side and add some weight to his. The glider immediately responds by speeding up. You stumble slightly, and the glider speeds up yet more as all your weight is added to it. You maintain your hold a moment too long and find yourself in the air over the edge, hanging on by your fingertips. Your light-hearted attempt at help has now put you in a potentially fatal situation.

Helping others

UP's Etsushi Matsuo (left) has the experience to handle this launch situation safely, but an enthusiastic novice could easily make things worse by grabbing the parachute handle!

As a general principle, give help when asked, otherwise be cautious. Naturally, you must not let this note of caution about helping stop you from acting positively if a really dangerous situation arises and you are in a position to do something about it.

If you yourself would really like help, ask for it before you attempt to launch, and tell the helper exactly what you require. It is probably wiser to decide to wait until conditions have calmed down and you can launch unaided.

Overhead electric cables

Overhead wires can be a big problem for paraglider pilots — particularly when setting up a landing in a previously unknown field after a cross-country flight. The danger is not usually the major groups of pylon-supported lines, which are easily seen, but smaller ones serving villages or farms. You can reduce the chance of flying into them by vigilance and a healthy sense of suspicion. Develop the habit of expecting every farm to have at least one wire leading to it, not necessarily following roads or field boundaries, and don't relax until you have found it. Don't even relax then — there may be another! Look for the poles, and remember that copper wire will have oxidized to a nice green which will make it invisible over grass when viewed from above. If there is an isolated barn or shed, look for the wire that powers the lighting or the milking machine.

If you have the misfortune to fly into wires and find yourself conscious and tangled up clear of the ground, do nothing except shout to keep well-meaning potential helpers away from you until there is absolutely no doubt that the power is off, no matter how long the wait may be.

If you see someone else hit wires and get hung up, forget heroics immediately. The first priority is for the electricity company to switch the power off. Unless you can easily find their own emergency number, call the general emergency number (999 in the UK, 911 in the USA) for the police or fire service, who will contact them for you. Under no circumstances must you attempt a rescue yourself until the line is safe. Keep ladders and ropes well away!

And finally, if an accident brings a wire which might be live into contact with the ground near you, move away by 'bunny hopping' with both feet together. That way you won't get a charge from the ground electrocuting you by flowing up one leg and down the other, as it may do if you stride away. No kidding.

Getting the paraglider down where you want to every time is active safety, yet I have frequently been to popular sites in continental Europe and seen people missing the landing area and arriving on the road, in trees and bushes, in backyards, and sometimes a couple of fields away. In some cases there is a valid excuse, when a valley wind switches 180° with the pilot committed to the final glide, but usually the reason is simply bad planning and lack of thought. The pilots get to the vicinity of the landing area and then hope to find a neat way of landing in it.

Here is a method which removes guesswork and works quite well. It deviates somewhat from most flying textbooks, because they are usually aimed at aircraft with much flatter glide angles and higher airspeeds than ours, and assume quite a long final approach with a straight glide over the threshold of the field. With the method described here, you make the final turn on or even within the threshold. This example assumes a field of at least 350 × 200 ft (100 × 60 m) in size and in exclusive use by paragliders. It also assumes that there are no particular local rules about land which you must not overfly.

You lose height during the downwind leg to one side of the field with a few gentle 360s or S-turns, always taking care to keep speed on to avoid stalling. When down to 50–60 ft (15–20 m) turn into the field and complete the landing. The advantage is that you can monitor the wind by watching your drift during the turns, and can even change your direction of landing at a relatively late stage if you decide that you have got it wrong at

Landing choices

Figure 26: Keeping your options open when approaching a landing field

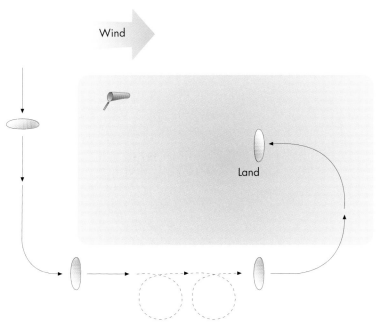

Wind

Land

first. You also avoid the embarrassing problem of underestimating the valley wind and finding yourself sinking vertically into the downwind field with everyone standing round the windsock and saying 'S/he's not going to make it!'.

Your landing planning should start a long way away from touchdown: take stock of any other gliders who are likely to be landing at about the same time and keep an eye on them. Then decide from which direction you will *probably* need to make your final approach.

Tree landings

Tree arrivals would be a better heading really; after all, by the very nature of the event it will not be exactly what you planned by way of a landing. There are two phases to a typical tree landing: hitting the tree and getting out of it. If you have any say in the matter, it is better to hit the tree fair and square in the middle of the branches and stay there, rather than hooking it on one side and being swung down to the ground from a great height. When impact becomes inevitable, protect your eyes with your forearms and try to keep your legs together. As soon as the crashing subsides, take stock of your situation and do nothing in a rush. Unless you are quite sure that you are likely to be cast to the ground at any second, the best action may be to sit tight and blow the whistle, which you will suddenly be very glad you had in your pocket. With any luck, helpers with rope and ladders will soon be on the way.

Only if you are absolutely confident that you can climb down safely, should you attempt to unclip from the wing. Do this by unhooking the karabiners rather than by getting out of the harness, because if you have guessed wrongly and later have to be lowered down by helpers, the harness will be very useful. However, watch out for snagging your reserve parachute handle on anything on the way down. Deploying it at this stage will not enhance your day.

Remember that a drop of only 10 or 15 ft (3–5 m) can cause a lot of damage. After you've been flying, perhaps at several thousand feet, it may not look much, but do reflect that more injuries are caused by falling out of trees than by flying into them.

If you have landed in a large forest, be sure to mark the trail so that you can find your way back to the tree and reclaim your wing. Use pieces of broken line, a torn-up neckscarf or something like that — not your rucksack or harness, which might be subsequently picked up by a thief or a well-meaning hiker. Get all the help you can to recover the paraglider: having several people to lift and pull branches can often make all the difference between a wrecked canopy and an intact one.

Accident reports

If you have an accident, file a report! Others must be allowed to learn from your misfortunes. Many national associations publish accident statistics, but these are only of value if they are truly comprehensive. Good statistics allow trends to be spotted before they become epidemics. For example, a line break on your glider may be due to having snagged it on a rock, but if the line in the same position breaks on half a dozen examples of the same model, there may be a manufacturing fault. Without your reports it could pass undetected for years.

When doubt creeps in

Sooner or later all pilots find themselves in the position of having to decide whether the conditions are fit to fly in or not. Weigh all the factors and make a good decision. If you don't get it right, you may find these words rattling across your consciousness as you struggle against the elements. They are probably as old as flying itself:

'It is far better to be down here wishing you were up there, than up there wishing you were down here.'

Coping with collapses

In Chapter 3 the possibility of a wingtip tucking under during flight was mentioned (see page 53). As your flying experience builds up you will become accustomed to occasional encounters with local turbulence which set your canopy shaking and your heart-rate shifting down a gear. Because paragliders are designed and tested to resist collapses, it is usually over almost before you have noticed it, and you fly on without having to take any action. Sometimes it can be rougher and you may look up to see the front of the wing tucking or a tip deflating and waving back at you. If you are flying a wing correctly suited to your experience, you still won't need to do anything except watch it resume its normal comforting shape within a second or two and without any input from you. But *suppose*, just for a moment, that it didn't recover on its own: would you really know exactly what to do?

The exercises on a typical SIV course equip you to handle such incidents and emergencies by requiring you to perform collapses and then extricate yourself from them. While writing this book I performed several of the SIV tasks on my own glider, under the tutelage of my son Rob, and expected to benefit by gaining extra technical piloting skills. That certainly happened, but the biggest benefit was the increase in confidence that followed. After undertaking SIV, you understand just how powerfully your paraglider wants

Simulation d'incident en vol (SIV)

Facing page: *Walter Holtzmuller (Austria) with his competition glider in a perfect B-line stall (see page 157)*

153

to stay in the air and how a little cool thinking can prevent a minor inconvenience from turning into a disaster.

Incorrectly executed, deflations and stalls are dangerous manoeuvres, and I stress that you *must not* experiment with them on your own. SIV must be done under controlled conditions with the guidance of a thoroughly trusted and qualified instructor. You need plenty of height, water underneath with a rescue boat standing by, a buoyancy jacket and a radio. Reject courses which have any one of these elements missing.

This book is not the place to instruct you on any of the techniques: the following comments are just to give you an impression of what you will encounter when your turn for an SIV course comes along. Any of my personal comments here relate to the Firebird 'Marlin', a very stable and forgiving intermediate glider — this should be borne in mind if you aspire to a hotter model.

Big ears ...

... and really big ears

Big ears

This is the mildest of all the manoeuvres, and is scarcely a part of the SIV range. Big ears simply consists of folding in the tips of the wing by pulling the outer one or two A-lines on each side. This reduces the area and efficiency of the wing and increases its sink rate — and, usually, its speed — so it is a common way of descending. You steer by weightshift while the ears are in. If you have flown at any popular site, you will almost certainly have seen someone 'pulling the ears' to make a top-landing.

It is a useful trick to know, not simply because it may come in useful, but also because it introduces you to the concept of deliberately collapsing part of your flying machine and then re-inflating it. I believe that all modern gliders can safely be big-earsed, but a few of the early ones could not. Don't go folding the tips in unless your handbook says it is OK.

Front tucks

The full front tuck is surprisingly undramatic, but it does require an act of will-power to pull firmly and evenly on both front risers to initiate it the first time. Dammit, all your flying so far has depended on those ports at the front of the cells remaining open, and here you go closing them with a couple of thousand feet of vacant space below you. Then you give a strong pull down on the risers, there is some vigorous rattling from the sail, a bit of penduluming and a reassuring whump! when you let the risers up again with as much control as you can muster and an undeniable feeling of relief. You will probably have just damped the penduluming nicely with a judicious touch of both brakes when the radio bleats at you: 'Not bad, but this time go a bit deeper and try to hold it for a bit longer — and look at the wing while you are doing it!'

After good symmetrical front tucks, the next item on the menu is usually asymmetrical ones, achieved by hauling on one or other of the A-risers. These look dreadful at first, but are easily cured by releasing the riser and possibly helping the re-inflation with a pump of the appropriate brake.

At this stage you will be following the advice to look at the wing during the manoeuvres, and finding that the sense of height and isolation disappears. You are now concerned just with the wing and your actions, a world limited to the length of the lines. There is a danger in this, as you can forget to monitor your altitude or the proximity of other gliders. Even when under instruction, you must keep a good lookout.

Stalls

Stalls will be somewhere on the SIV agenda: perhaps you will be told to take the glider to the edge of a full stall by taking both brakes far below hip level, waiting for the wing to start to deform and then releasing them steadily just before it folds back. The glider will slow down considerably during this, and you will swing back and forwards quite a lot during the recovery.

B-lining

Maybe you will do the so-called B-line stalls, illustrated on page 152. B-lining is simple, and is one of the SIV tasks which could have a practical application if you get into irresistible lift — it is a way of getting down quickly. Just reach up to the top of the B-risers and pull them down towards your shoulders. This is easier said than done, because the effort required is great. You will probably find that you need to hook a finger or two into the lines where they meet the top of the riser and virtually heave yourself out of the seat before the whole undersurface of the wing 'breaks' across its width and you become conscious that the relative airflow is up your trouser legs rather than into your face. My shoulder joints are unreliable, so I find B-lining very uncomfortable. After a few seconds of descent, you let the pressure off steadily and the glider resumes normal flight. I experienced absolutely no problems in exiting from the B-line stall, but some models of glider are liable to go directly into a stabilized stall if the risers are released too gently.

Full stall

The full stall used to be included in SIV courses, but it is a distinctly dangerous procedure without a truly predictable outcome. When it began to be realized that in everyday flying full stalls are virtually unknown, but

A very fully developed stall

that practising them deliberately was causing several accidents each year, common sense prevailed and the teaching of the manoeuvre has now ceased. I'll tell you what it's like so that it won't remain a complete mystery, but please don't try it — full stalls are so risky that not even the vastly experienced AFNOR test pilots include it in their repertoires.

Briefly, the pilot takes a wrap or two on each brake, and then slows the glider right down before finally pulling the brakes on to their fullest extent and holding them there with the arms locked straight down beside the thighs. The wing reacts by folding backwards in a horseshoe shape and flapping and rattling mightily. The descent rate is considerable, but the whole procedure is relatively stable at this stage.

The drama starts when the pilot lets the brakes back up again. If this is done smoothly and symmetrically, the wing should start flying again, although it will surge forwards, probably violently, and there will be a lot of penduluming. If the gods are not smiling or at least grinning a little, the wing surges so viciously that it flies forwards under the pilot, who promptly plummets into it. The remainder of the flight is brief and well outside the scope of any curriculum.

Instead of teaching the full stall, most responsible instructors now concentrate on teaching their pupils appreciation of slow flight and the onset of a partial stall.

Spirals and spins

Other components of an SIV course are the spiral dive and the spin.

The *spiral* is simply a succession of tight 360° turns in which you can eventually reach a bank angle approaching 90° accompanied by a formidable rate of descent. The main hazards of this are disorientation and clumsiness in restoring everything to straight and level flight.

The *flat spin* is an altogether nastier animal in which the wing is part-collapsed on one side, with the inflated side rotating around it. As the wing can rotate faster than the pilot, the brake lines and risers twist together to form a short cord, and after a few turns, the brakes become inoperative. I cannot suggest a cure for this, as the only spin I was rash enough to become involved with was arrested after three turns and it was simply a matter of reaching up to assist in the untwisting when everything seemed to be about the right way up again. Throwing the reserve is an option, but doing this needs a little care and luck if it is not to become twisted around the paraglider as it deploys. The standard advice is to throw the reserve in the opposite direction to the spin.

This tip seems to be fairly permanently tangled, but fortunately the glider is still operating well. Liechtenstein champion Martin Buhler seems to be remarkably unconcerned. When the canopy is caught up in the lines like this, the effect is often described as a cravate.

Rob in a spiral on a Ninja

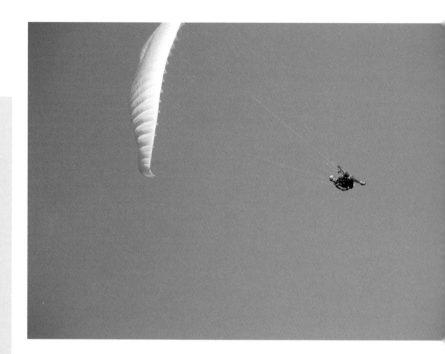

There is no formal agreement about the exact content of an SIV course. Quite apart from the obvious physical dangers, an over-ambitious course can be as bad for your flying confidence as none at all. There is a fine line between executing radical manoeuvres which will equip you better in the event of trouble in your everyday flying, and attempting those which are strictly in the realm of professional test-pilots. Always choose a course with qualified instructors who are prepared to tailor their demands to your capabilities and ambitions. If a course seems to be turning into a competition to see who can get away with the most radical manoeuvres, respect your own judgement and have nothing more to do with it. Don't laugh, it happens!

With all the manoeuvres, nothing very complicated is required from the pilot to restore normal flying service, but with practice you can improve your performance considerably. At first you won't have a clear idea of which way you are pointing during the exercises, and in the open space over a big lake this is not too important. However, if you have to cope with a deflation while attempting to thermal alongside a mountain, the ability to handle it and exit in an appropriate direction is vital. As Rob Whittall says, 'There's no point in recovering from a stall if you then fly straight into a cliff.' With practice, however, you will find that you can recover smoothly and on the correct heading.

SIV hazards

- Repeated violent manoeuvres will load your glider to the extent that it will wear out more quickly. So will soaking it and having it heaved out of the water into a boat.

- You can become so engrossed in the manoeuvres, all of which use — or lose — lots of height, that you can find the landing field is beyond reach at the end of a session.

CHAPTER 10

Most collapses are fairly minor and easy to recover from, and the SIV activities teach you not to panic if the paraglider suddenly changes shape. However, there is a world of difference between collapses which you induce and those which arrive unannounced.

Here are some basic tips for getting everything under control again:

- The brake controls do more than steer: they double as pumps to shift air about *inside* the wing.

- Collapses are recovered by pumping. Think of the paraglider wing as a set of huge bellows, and use the brake controls to pump air from one part to another. The holes in the cell dividers allow air to reach every part, unassisted by Heineken. Quick little jabs at the controls are a waste of time — you need long, firm pumps to get the air moving.

- If you have a tip collapse — this is the most common event — counter the extra drag on that side by applying some brake on the opposite side to keep you flying straight. Then sort out the deflation by pumping as necessary.

- If the collapse occurs while you are activating a speed system, release the pressure on the stirrup quickly but smoothly. If the problem is a front collapse, this alone will often cure it.

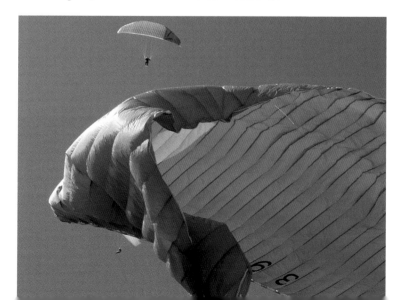

A massive tip collapse during launch. If this happens while you still have the option of aborting the take-off and starting again, you should do so.

- Which control to pump? It all depends on which parts of the glider remain inflated. If it's just a small deflation, apply a little opposite brake to counter any turn, and then use a couple of long pumps on the deflated side to get the wing back into shape again. If half the wing has collapsed and folded under, you need to pump the *opposite* control to get air across into the deflated side, perhaps followed by a smaller pump or two on the collapsed side to bring the tip into shape. This second case is quite extreme, and is included here to show that you have to think about what you are doing — there are times when simple rules such as 'pump the deflated side' won't work.

- Wind strength and direction can play a big part in the ease of recovery, so if you are trying to re-inflate in a strong crosswind, don't expect exactly the same response that you got in the calm air over the lake.

- Expect the wing to snap back into shape quite vigorously, and be ready to damp out the resulting swing by judicious use of the brakes.

- If you find that you are experiencing repeated partial collapses while thermalling, don't automatically blame the glider or the conditions. Could you be flying too slowly?

Parachute deployments

The emergency parachute is a haven of last resort. If you do have to throw one, don't expect a smooth ride. Assuming it doesn't tangle with the flapping remains of your paraglider, it will open with a jerk and you will probably be swung from side to side as it oscillates. If you are swinging, you will have no say about what part of the arc you will be passing through when the ground arrives. You will almost certainly not be able to choose your landing field, and will be lucky to steer away from trees or power lines. The descent rate will be amazingly rapid compared with the paraglider you are used to. Never be tempted to throw the 'chute to see what happens!

CHAPTER 10

Cross-country flying

Soaring on a ridge or repeating circuits of a tow-launch airfield is great sport, but after a while many pilots feel that they want to take the freedom of the air to greater limits. After learning to fly in the first place, the next great adventure lies in trying to cover the miles to a distant landing place. All you need are some thermalling skills (Chapter 7) and good knowledge of any airspace restrictions on your course (Chapter 13). A little courage comes in handy too.

First cross-countries

Cross-country success depends upon becoming established in a thermal that is strong enough to get you away from your launch area — and preferably to take you close to cloudbase. Imagine that you climb 2,000 ft (600 m) in a wind of 10 mph (17 kph), and remain at about that height under the cloud at the top of the thermal for ten minutes, before flying on in a straight downwind glide during which you encounter no more lift at all: by the time you land you will have covered at least 5 miles (8 km), quite enough to qualify as a genuine cross-country. Finding another thermal could easily have doubled the distance.

This style of downwind flight is typical of distance flying in much of the British Isles, where the hills are low and the wind a normal feature. The difficult point is making the original decision that this is the thermal to go with. I am a champion at saying to myself 'there'll be a better one soon, I need a thousand feet to leave with, I'll fly back to the ridge for now' when I am circling and am at decision-point, perhaps 700 ft up. The really successful pilots don't worry about how high (or low) they are; provided they are established in the lift, they just stay with it and go.

Among mountains it can be easier. Here, typical cross-countries are flown by hopping along ranges, from one spur to another. There is often a thermal on each spur which gives enough height to reach the next one. The big challenges come when it is time to try to cross valleys or other big gaps.

Nice view. Pity about the footwear …

Reaching cloudbase is very satisfying, and it can be rather surprising the first few times. You will feel the moisture in the air before you get to the clouds, and then may find that you are becoming engulfed. It is common to have good visibility directly downwards, but not much sideways. This is because the undersides of cumulus clouds are often concave and you are in the hollow bit. The lift can continue right up into the clouds, fed by the latent heat released by condensation, so be prepared to fly to one side if it is getting too strong, or even to pull 'big ears' to increase the sink rate.

CROSS-COUNTRY FLYING

In cross-country flying, height equals distance, so remain flying fairly slowly in very weak lift or zero sink rather than rushing on into the unknown. If you run into sink, unless you are really confident of finding another thermal, fly downwind at best-glide speed. Slow down again as soon as there is any hint of lift. Paragliders are great thermalling aircraft, but are woefully poor when it comes to covering the ground to the next thermal source or cloud. Be prepared to lose all your hard-won height in a single cross-wind track to a possible lift source, and don't be too disappointed if there is nothing there.

Landing fields

One of the great keys to success at cross-country lies in detaching your thoughts from the ground and concentrating on the flying. The sound of the vario and the condition of the sky are what is important. However, this must not occupy you to the extent that you forget the basic rule of always having a possible landing field within reach. This is a constant, almost subconscious,

A glorious situation: altitude of 3,000 ft (1000 m) or more, and safe fields as far as the eye can see ...

occupation, and while you still have plenty of height you don't need to be too specific; it is enough to note that you can comfortably clear a forest and reach a selection of fields beyond it. Once you are down to six or seven hundred feet (200 m), though, you have to make some good decisions quite fast. From here you will probably be on the ground in two minutes, and your choices will be very limited. Always choose a field without livestock in it if you possibly can. Watch for powerlines like a hawk; if you can make life easier for yourself by landing near the road, so much the better, but don't let such considerations take precedence over a big safe field with a good approach.

Paraglider pilots setting off on first cross-countries and landing after one thermal are causing problems at some of the popular flying sites because they frequently land in the same field a few miles away. Farmers are generally quite tolerant of occasional outlandings on their land, but when it happens time after time it can become a problem. Check with the club site officer if there are any sensitive areas to avoid just downwind of your launch area, and don't be surprised if the farmer doesn't share your 'first XC euphoria' when you land among his sheep.

Too much too soon?
Suppose it is a fabulous day, with the thermals perfectly spaced so that you can fly from one to another so easily that you are out of your county in an hour or less. You are in unknown country and can apparently stay up for ever, so what should you do? Land! If you don't know where you are, there is a very real chance of blundering into controlled airspace. Even if you are carrying a map, it is no good if you are lost. Accurate navigation is just as important a part of cross-country flying as the ability to fly.

Extra comforts

Cross-country flying inevitably involves retrieves and a lot of time waiting around. Carry some food and drink, and small change for the phone. In densely populated temperate countries such as Britain the drink will just make life more pleasant, but in many parts of the world it is an essential life-saver.

Radio

Once you become seriously involved in flying away from the hill, you will start to think about getting a radio and keeping in contact with fellow fliers and retrieve crews. The legal way to do this in the UK is on Airband, where we are encouraged to use 129.9 MHz, the glider frequency. This is the only form of radio which you are allowed to transmit with while airborne. Airband sets are quite expensive.

Two-metre-band hand-held radios are available for ground use by licensed radio amateurs in the UK, and the quality of transmission and reception on these is excellent. Unfortunately the exam you have to pass to obtain a licence is unrealistically complex, although there are evening classes in many areas if you are really determined. Two-metres are popular for retrieve use in countries where there is more freedom of the airwaves. Whatever radio you use, respect the protocols and keep speech to the minimum.

Cellphones are a useful retrieve tool, at a price; CB radio, in my experience, is virtually useless.

If electronic communication fails to connect you with your lift after a cross-country flight, try the old idea of carrying a card saying 'GLIDER PILOT' as a hitch-hiking aid. It still works well.

Competition flying

Competition flying is a big part of the paragliding scene. Involvement creeps up on you almost without your noticing it: perhaps you will find yourself on the hillside at the end of a day and someone will suggest trying to fly back to the car park. Suddenly a routine flight down becomes a test of skill in stretching the glide as far as possible. Maybe you will get lucky and find a lingering blob of lift which takes you a few metres nearer to the cars than anyone else. You won! This gives the ego a pleasant boost and could lure you into entering your club's competition a couple of weeks later. After a few more club comps, a couple of modest attempts in the cross-country listings and entry into your national league, you may start thinking of venturing abroad to your first international competitions. It is fair to add that if this all seems like a tempting prospect, anyone close to you should see it as a threat … competition flying absorbs lots of time and substantial sums of money.

Competition can mean simple tasks such as spot-landing or attempting touch-and-goes in a designated area, but the real sport starts when cross-country tasks are introduced. This means that are a number of different skills to test, and if you want to be a successful competition pilot, you will have to master all of them. Apart from good thermalling ability, you need to be able to navigate accurately, to plan the best time to launch, and to keep a cool head when surrounded on all sides by other gliders. You also have to use a camera in the air to record turnpoints, and be prepared to deal with the form-filling and reporting that are all part of the game.

Rob launches an Ozone Proton during the 1999 World Championships in Austria. The Proton is a 'series production' class glider rather than an unrestricted racer. There is increasing emphasis on safety in competition.

Not long ago, paragliding competition simply meant seeing who could fly furthest on the day. Now performance has improved so much that tasks are set which involve flying to a goal, and usually there will be one or two turnpoints along the way which will mean that some of the course will be across-wind. To win, it's not enough to get to goal — you have to get there fast.

International competitions

The pinnacle of competition is the FAI World Championships. This is held every other year, and up to 180 competitors will take part in the two weeks of tasks. There are awards for the top individuals and teams. At the time of writing the women's championship is part of the main event, but there is some discussion about holding a completely separate women's event. FAI Continental Championships are held in the alternate years. Entrants for these events are normally selected by the national associations of the competing countries.

The Paragliding World Cup is a series of events which is organized each year by the PWC Committee. Rounds are held in many countries, and often there is a qualifying day or two in which anyone with a competition licence can participate. This is a good way to start in large-scale competitions.

A race-to-goal championship day

Here's a look at a typical day at a big international championship:

0800 hrs Team Leaders attend a meeting. The previous day's results are handed out and a weather briefing is given. The Meet Director announces the site for the day and sets the time for departure of the pilots' buses at 0845. Meanwhile the competitors collect their films for the day, packed lunches, and special emergency radios whose batteries have been recharging overnight.

0900 hrs The buses finally get away.

A good 'meteo' briefing is an essential part of a successful competition.

1030 hrs Arrive at the mountain top. The wind is light and coming from behind the launch area. However, the sun will get onto the slope soon, so launching should be possible as soon as thermal activity starts.

1035 hrs The Meet Director announces that there will be a briefing at 1100 hrs.

1100 hrs The wind is no longer coming over the back. The Meet Director announces the task as a race to goal at Bigtown Racecourse, via a single turnpoint at Smalltown slaughterhouse. The distance is 50 km. The launch window will open at 1200 hrs, and the start point will be activated at 1300 hrs.

The organizers have provided a very comprehensive information board here. Competitors have to take a photo of the task board (on the right) each day, on the same roll of film that will contain their turnpoint photos. Sample turnpoint shots are provided, so that the pilots know exactly what they have to look for.

The pilots now know what they will have to do. They take the required photographs of the task board and make their way to the launch area. There's no great hurry, because nobody can launch before noon.

Pure race tasks are not timed from take-off, but from a start point which is usually in the vicinity of the launch area but lower

The British team discussing the task and plotting possible routes before the window opens

down the hillside. Beside the start point will be a large coloured cloth square (the tarpaulin, or *tarp* for short). This will be rolled up until the start activation time, when it will immediately be laid out flat. As soon as it is laid out, the pilots can photograph it from the air and set off along their course. Naturally, their photos have be taken from the correct side of the start point, and this will have been indicated at the briefing.

1200 hrs For this task the activation time is 1.00 pm, so all the pilots have an hour in which to launch and get into a good position to start the task. Some will elect to get off early so that they have the maximum time to gain altitude, while others will hang around on the ground, using the early fliers to mark the thermals and generally give them a feel for the conditions.

1255 hrs With five minutes left, there are only a couple of stragglers left on the ground — all the 120-odd other competitors are crowding the air waiting for the tarp to open. This can be a spectacular sight! Then a horn blows, the tarp opens and the race is on.

It will probably take the fastest competitors about two hours to reach the distant goal, and it's sometimes possible to watch the start and then drive to the finish. Often the road takes you along the valley while the competitors pick their way from thermal to thermal above the mountain tops. You get tantalizing glimpses which tell you that the pilots are well on the way, but often they are too distant to identify accurately. This all adds to the excitement.

At a well-organized event the goal field will be staffed by several experienced observers. The goal line will be clearly marked so that the approaching pilots can see it from a kilometre or more away, and there will be at least a couple of windsocks. If you have arrived early, it can be hard to imagine that anyone will reach here on a paraglider. From time to time everyone scans the air in the general direction of the last turnpoint. Then a later arrival in a car rushes up and announces 'There's a couple about 5k back — don't know who', and several pairs of binoculars sweep the sky again. Soon two distant dots become intermittently visible as the sunlight catches them when they turn. Look away for a moment and you'll lose them. It takes more than a quarter of an hour for the first to reach the line — still so high that he has to circle a few times before he is low enough for the timekeepers to get his number as he crosses. As soon as he's down to about 650 ft (200 m), a flag is waved from the centre of the line and he is free to land anywhere nearby — to a round of applause, naturally. The second races in rather lower, and only a few seconds later.

From now on there are frequent bursts of action as small groups are spotted in the distance. This is going to be a day when lots of pilots reach goal. There are cheers when one glider scrapes over the line with less than a couple of metres to spare, and groans as another lands a field away without making it.

A strong team of spotters and recorders keeping check on goal arrivals

CHAPTER 12

Judging the final glide on such a slow aircraft as a paraglider is extremely difficult. The first pilot home was wise to keep plenty of height in hand, because a single unexpected area of sink or headwind could easily have robbed him of the goal. The one following had the advantage of being able to see how the leader was doing and to adjust speed and glide angle accordingly.

For spectators, this race task has a big advantage in that it is easy to understand: the competitors arrive at goal in their finishing order. Everyone knows at once who has won, which is far from the case in some other tasks. In the next section we take a closer look at tasks and how they are scored.

Tasks and scoring systems

Scoring the race-to-goal task described above is relatively simple, but for other cross-country tasks it can be very complex. The formulas used have been developed from the other soaring sports of gliding (sailplanes) and hang gliding. To my mind we have allowed things to get *too* complex, but we seem to be stuck with variations on the same theme, so I guess that something like the current systems will be around for a long time yet.

The problems

For competition to be fair, the competitors need to have equal chances to use their skills. In competitive soaring this is quite difficult to arrange, because the weather conditions can change so much during a task. This would not be such a problem if everybody could always take off exactly when they wished — launch decision would then be just another skill for successful pilots to master — but this is not often possible, due to restrictions on site size and the problems of ensuring timing accuracy at launch. There is also the problem that, assuming lift conditions are equal, a pilot who starts late will have the advantage that the thermals will be marked by those ahead of him. In hang-gliding competitions I have seen this be such a problem that the entire launch window was missed because nobody was prepared to take the initiative and go first.

How the scoring works

Basically, the scoring works by giving the winner of a day's task 1000 points and ranking everyone else in proportion to that, according to the distance they achieve and the time they take. The points are divided into distance points and time points, and the way they are divided can have a great effect on the way a pilot attacks a task. For example, if the split is 700 points for distance and 300 for time, a cautious approach which guarantees reaching goal would be sensible. If the split is the other way round, it may be worthwhile flying much more aggressively, because if you reach goal with a slow time you will not get a very high score at all. Of course, in either case you need to reach goal to make any sort of really respectable score!

What happens if you don't reach goal? Well, you simply get a proportion of the distance points, according to how much of the course you cover.

So far, so simple, but the scope for complicating matters is immense. The next step is to split the time points and relate half of them to the position of arrival at goal. The idea of this is to reward pilots who take the initiative and lead the way.

The next area for attention is the relative difficulty of the task: here the scoring-system experts have introduced yet another variable, the *round factor*. The thinking behind this is that the pilots should be better rewarded for a task that takes four hours than for one which is over and done with in forty minutes. It also overcomes the reluctance of some meet directors to set short tasks on days when the weather is poor.

In some systems the figures are fairly simple, say 1000 points for the winner of a long task and 700 for a short one; others use a sub-formula which takes into account the number of finishers and their average time. This latter method seems fair at first sight, but it has been known to work against a pilot who puts in a brilliant performance when everyone else does badly.

A big problem with these sophisticated scoring systems is that it takes quite a long time to process the results; often nobody knows who is winning until the next day. This deprives the public of any real sense of excitement in connection with paragliding competitions — after all, one of the main attractions of a sport is seeing who is winning and who is losing. It also makes life difficult for television crews to produce attractive features. Consequently people are always looking for fresh competition formats which will produce instant results while still testing the pilots fairly.

Cat's Cradle

Naturally, organizers try to find simpler ways of scoring tasks, and many variations have been tried. One is to designate a large number of turnpoints within a relatively small area and set the competitors to go around as many as possible, in any order but never the same one twice, within a given time. This is referred to a *Cat's Cradle* task. If the conditions are good it can work well, but it gives a lot of headaches to the people who have to check the competitor's films.

Cross-Country Classic

As a reaction to the very tightly defined tasks, the *Cross-Country Classic* system has evolved in the USA for hang gliding, and is being tried for paragliders too. Several turnpoints are defined, and the pilots can choose their own task, according to what they think is possible on the day. They can choose an out-and-return, a triangle, or simply a straight-line distance task, and can even change their minds part-way through if they find that their original choice is unattainable. Points are awarded according to distance flown — no timing is involved. Typically, there will be 1 point per mile for straight distance, 1.3 points per mile for an out-and-return, and 1.5 points per mile for a completed triangle.

Getting started in competition

If you are a member of any paragliding club, sooner or later you will get the opportunity to try your hand at competition. Have a go! No matter what sort of event it is, the following approach will help you to do your best:

- Fly a paraglider you are thoroughly familiar with. Don't buy or borrow a high-performer especially for the comp.

- Check everything the day before. If the rules and regulations have been printed in advance, read them thoroughly so that you know exactly what will be expected of you.

- Spend plenty of time familiarizing yourself with the map before you fly. Take particular trouble to visualize several features on the way to the goal, so that you avoid basic errors such as flying down the wrong valley.

- Mark your intended line of flight on your map.

- If you are going to need a camera to record turnpoints, practice using it with your flying gloves on before you get into the sky. That way you will discover whether you can operate the shutter and wind-on easily, and learn how to avoid taking extreme close-ups of your fingers.

Figure 27: The FAI turnpoint sector. Buildings make good features for turnpoints, because their vertical components make it easy to see which side the shot was taken from. Flat features such as road junctions are less satisfactory.

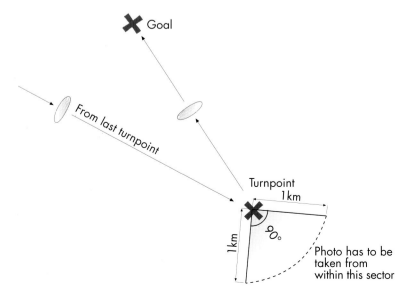

178

- Get your turn-point photos right! Failure here is a great mark-loser. You have to be within a kilometre of the turnpoint feature and in a 90° sector which is opposite the next leg of the task (see Figure 27).

- Have safety lines on everything: camera, vario, map-holder. Then check that the one on the camera is long enough to allow you to get your eye to the viewfinder.

- Turn up in good time on the day, and really listen to the briefings.

- Fly the task. For example, concentrate on getting to goal rather than racing to goal.

You can't realistically expect to win your first competition, but with a bit of intelligent flying a place in the top ten is not out of the question.

The complete competition pilot. Richard Gallon (France) girded up and ready to go.

- Do your own sums and have faith in them. Be realistic about the speed at which you hope to cover the course, and launch at a time which will give you a fair chance of finishing it. For example, on a light-wind day 15 kph (10 mph) is a good speed to average, so if a 60-km goal is set, make sure that you get off early enough to give you four hours in the air. Don't worry if the aces seem to be waiting for ever — go when *you* are ready. It may be that they really can average 25 kph, but it's more likely that they are psyching each other up.

- Respect your own judgement: don't just follow the crowd. It is not unknown for a dozen competitors in a world championship to photograph the same incorrect turnpoint simply because the leader did.

- Watch the weather all the time. Forecasts are only a guide. If your own observations suggest that the weather is ignoring the forecasters' instructions, make the most of the situation: many of your competitors will assume that the weather is doing exactly what they were told it would do, and will reject the evidence before their eyes.

- The rules for international competitions are published by the FAI. There are two booklets: *Sporting Code, General Section*, which lays down the basic procedures for all aviation competitions, and *Section 7*, which specifically applies to hang gliding and paragliding. These are not a very stimulating casual read, but if you are serious about competition they will represent time well invested.

- Paragliding is still a young sport with plenty of scope for new ideas and fresh approaches. If you think positively and have a flair for flying, you can be doing well in international events after only a season or two. Don't be afraid of winning!

Rules, laws and airspace

Flight is an immense freedom, but it is not an unlimited one. As soon as you take off in any type of aircraft, you are bound by the air laws of the country
you are flying over. In this sense, paragliders are no
different from any other type of flying machine. It is
essential that air laws are respected scrupulously if
we are to preserve reasonably wide limits to our
flying freedom.

Why have rules?

Before going on to the dry details of the rules and
regulations, consider the reasons behind some of
them:

- Aircraft must avoid collision at all costs.

- Almost anything falling from an aircraft is a threat to
  life underneath.

- All pilots are hampered by blind spots in their vision;
  paraglider pilots are better off in this respect than
  any others, but remember — just because you can
  see another aircraft, it doesn't mean that its pilot can
  necessarily see you.

- There are areas on the ground over which it would
  be dangerous to fly. Military firing ranges are an
  obvious example.

- Some people lack imagination to the extent that
  they will do really stupid things. Laws don't stop this,
  but they help a bit.

Air law worldwide

Although there is some conformity of air law through-out the world, and the object of ICAO is to increase this, there are significant differences, and it is the responsibility of all pilots to know and respect the rules which apply in the countries where they fly.

In the United Kingdom

The Air Navigation Order contains the umbrella of laws which apply to flight in the United Kingdom. As soon as you decide to fly a paraglider you become bound by these laws, although most of them are obviously drawn up with powered aircraft in mind. In the eyes of the law you are a 'commander of an air-craft', and as such you must accept certain legal responsibilities.

For example, you must satisfy yourself before take-off that 'all the equipment required for the flight is in a fit condition for use'. Therefore the pre-flight check is more than a good idea — it is a legal necessity. Once in the air you must not 'recklessly or negligently cause or permit an aircraft to endanger any person or prop-erty', so don't make a habit of buzzing the onlookers or soaring without keeping a proper look-out. You must not be under the influence of drink or drugs. Leave at least eight hours between any alcohol and flight — longer if you've really been partying.

Reference sources

A useful source of air-law facts is the small book published by the CAA, *CAP 85*. This is primarily for students entering the private pilot maze, but much of its contents are directly applicable to paragliding. It is a great help if you are taking the BHPA's pilot-rating exams. In this respect, the annual training issue of the BHPA's magazine *Skywings* is invaluable too.

The *UK Air Pilot* is the bible of flight in the British Isles. This is a weighty and expensive book which is updat-ed several times each year. Your nearest central library should keep a copy.

Basic rules

Facing page: *Both these pilots were safely within the appropriate airspace. The system depends upon all air users knowing exactly where they are.*

ATZ Aerodrome Traffic Zone

AIAA Area of Intense Aerial Activity

AMSL Above Mean Sea Level

ANO Air Navigation Order

CTA Control Area

CTR Control Zone

FIR Flight Information Region

FL Flight Level

IMC Instrument Meteorological Conditions

ICAO International Civil Aviation Organization

MATZ Military Aerodrome Traffic Zone

TMA Terminal Manoeuvring Area

VFR Visual Flight Rules

VMC Visual Meteorological Conditions

The information in this chapter is an overview only. It applies to unpowered aircraft — you cannot add an engine and still enjoy the privileges of a glider.

Anti-collision rules

This is a refresher for the rules given on page 61. These rules are simple, and you *must* know them and use them instinctively:

1 Aircraft flying towards each other — **break right.**

2 Aircraft on converging courses — **the aircraft on the right has priority;** the other one must change course.

3 Overtaking a slower aircraft while ridge soaring in the UK — **pass between the other aircraft and the ridge**. (In other countries the opposite is often true: you may find it is customary to pass outside the slower aircraft, but leave plenty of room.)

4 On approach and landing — **the lower aircraft has priority.**

5 Powered aircraft give way to gliders and everyone gives way to balloons. However, be realistic, and remember that overall it is the pilot's responsibility to do everything possible to avoid collision.

Abbreviations

Aviation jargon is as littered with abbreviations as a dairy pasture with cow-muck. You never stop tripping over new ones, but the panel lists some of those you need to know for a start.

Units

On aeronautical charts, in line with international aviation convention, heights are measured in feet, horizontal distances in metres and kilometres or nautical miles, and speeds in knots. Sport pilots in Europe tend to use metres for height and metres per second for speed.

Aeronautical charts

To fly legally, you must not stray into controlled air-space. When you are at your local club's site, ridge soaring or doing circuits from the towline, you should not have any problems. However, as soon as you start to think about cross-country flight, even in the form of quite short hops, you need to know where you can fly.

The information is all on the aeronautical charts, which in the UK are published by the CAA. Your first sight of one of these 'air maps' can be a daunting experience, leaving you with the impression that the entire country is covered by an invisible labyrinth of such complexity that you will never make sense of it. Can this possibly be that same deserted open sky that you have been scraping around near the bottom of during the weekends of the last year or so? 'Fraid so, but persevere! Much of the labyrinth is at heights which you are unlikely to achieve, and once you have gained a little knowledge of what the symbols and abbreviations on the chart mean, you will soon make sense of it.

Don't imagine that you have to commit the whole lot to memory. The chart is a reference source which you should use frequently. Until you can contemplate really long cross-country flights, you will do better to transfer its information onto a local map with a larger scale, rather than trying to read it in flight. The key at the bottom of the map sheets contains loads of useful information, and unless you are map-reading almost daily, you will need to freshen up your knowledge from it quite often.

The charts are quite large and it is not unknown for pilots to cut the bottom part off to make them more manageable. This is usually regretted later.

Classification of airspace

It is impossible to cover all the intricacies of air charts in a book such as this, but here is a start:

How the air is carved up

Just a fraction of an aero-nautical chart, reproduced at half size. Some practice is needed to become familiar with the symbols. Can you identify the hang-gliding sites near the bottom of the sample?

In many countries (including the UK and the USA), airspace is classified under the ICAO system. This has seven categories, defined in terms of the access regulations. However, some countries do not use them all, and their implementations can and do vary, so always check. The categories are marked on the charts by the class letter boxed in blue.

The descriptions that follow apply to the UK.

Class A All the major airways. The flight levels of these are given on the chart, and it is usually possible to fly safely underneath them. The rules for general access to Class A airspace are complex and depend on the use of radio for contact with air-traffic controllers. In spite of all this, gliders, including paragliders, may be allowed to cross certain airways in VMC (see page 195), provided that they take the shortest crossing route and refrain from circling. The airways in Britain to which this concession applies are published in the *UK Air Pilot*, but as a relatively inexperienced paraglider pilot, you are well advised to keep out of them completely.

Class B Effectively this is all airspace above flight level 245 (think of it as 24,500 ft), so don't stay awake worrying about what you will meet if you stray into it one day.

Class C There is no Class C airspace over the UK, but you can find some in Eire where it appears frequently as the lower part of Airways and Control Areas. As Air Traffic Control clearance is required to enter Class C airspace, it is effectively closed to us.

Class D A common category covering many Control Areas and Control Zones around regional commercial airports. You may enter several of these without prior permission, provided that you are operating in VMC (see page 195). Each year, in *Skywings* magazine, the BHPA publishes a list of those areas in the UK that may be entered in this manner. Do not confuse the right to enter a CTR or CTA with the need to keep out of the smaller Aerodrome Traffic Zone (ATZ) within it.

Class E Belfast TMA and most of the Scottish TMA. Class E may be entered under similar conditions for VMC as listed under Class D above, except that the flight-visibility requirement is relaxed to 5 km.

Class F Advisory airspace. You can think of these as low-grade airways in which all the traffic will be flying according to VFR. You have free access to this, but must be extra-vigilant for commercial traffic. This airspace is shown by single lines on the chart, but you should visualize the routes as being normal airway width.

Class G The rest! You may fly freely here provided you take account of all the other users and of the mass of restricted space such as that above small airfields, military airfields and Danger Areas — see next section — which share Class G. The rule is: **see and be seen.**

Other areas of restriction

By the time you read through the list from A to G, you could be forgiven for thinking that must be everything. Unfortunately there are all sorts of other hazards about which you must be aware. Again, the details given here apply to the United Kingdom.

Aerodrome Traffic Zones (ATZ)

Think of these as transparent vertical cylinders 2,000 ft high, centred on the longest runway. If that runway is less than 1,850 metres long, the zone will have a radius of 2 nautical miles. If the runway is longer, the radius will be 2.5 nautical miles. I wonder if you find this wild mixture of units as irritating as I do? You cannot glide into or through an ATZ without air-traffic control clearance.

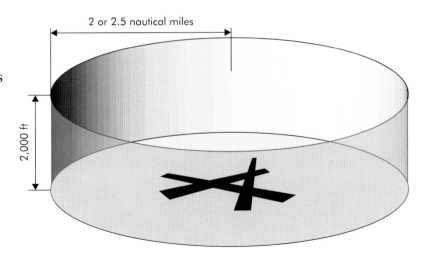

Figure 28: Aerodrome Traffic Zones (ATZ)

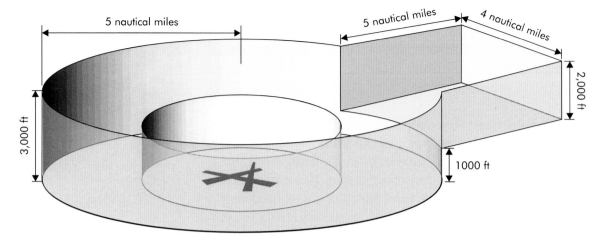

Military Aerodrome Traffic Zones (MATZ)

Military airfields have an ATZ of similar size to civil ones, but this is surrounded by a larger zone designated a MATZ. Typically, these are 3,000 ft high and 5 nautical miles in radius. In addition there will be an aerial stub 4 nautical miles wide and 5 nautical miles long which extends the MATZ in line with its principal runway (see Figure 29). Gliders are permitted to enter MATZs, but when you realize that the air is likely to be full of novice fighter-pilots flying state-owned equipment, it may not seem like a very good idea. The good news is that MATZs are frequently inoperative at weekends and national holidays. Don't gamble on this, though — your club should have details.

The rules and restrictions in this section apply only to unpowered paragliders. Powered versions (PPGs) must respect greater airspace limitations which are detailed in a special exemption granted by the CAA.

Prohibited Areas (P), Restricted Areas (R), Danger Areas (D) and Weapons Range Danger Areas (WRDA)

These are the spaces above military firing and exercise areas and hazardous industrial plants such as nuclear reactors. They are easy to identify on the chart, and their effective altitude above mean sea level is indicated by the figure after the reference number. This gives the altitude in thousands of feet.

It does not require deductive genius to work out that you should not enter a Prohibited Area under any circumstances. Restricted Areas have a little more flexibility, but you must still steer well clear of them unless you know exactly what the restriction is.

Strictly speaking, Ds and WRDAs are areas you are simply *advised* to avoid, unless they have a asterisk (*) in front of the number on the chart, in which case there are by-laws prohibiting entry during active periods. In the UK, full details of timings can be found in the relevant section of the *UK Air Pilot*. Apart from the in-the-air risks connected with overflying these areas, you need to know exactly where they are and be confident of not landing in them because of the danger from unexploded ordnance — this is in addition to the wrath of the authorities and the bad reputation you get for the sport. If in doubt — keep out!

'Microwaves'

This is the casual name for High Intensity Radio Transmission Areas (HIRTAs). On the chart they look like small Danger areas, but if you take a second look you will see that they are hatched all over, rather than shaded at the edges. The figure after the name indicates the effective height AMSL. If you find your variometer apparently going crazy part-way through a cross-country flight, it could be due to the emissions from a HIRTA — they can be powerful enough to scramble instruments. Check the chart!

Non-ATZ airfields
The chart will reveal all sorts of bases for aerial activity such as gliding centres, microlight fields, farmers' airstrips, bird sanctuaries and so on. You need to be able to identify all of these and to respect the users.

You also have to take care when overflying built-up areas and large gatherings of people. Briefly, with built-up areas the rule is that you must keep at such a height that you can glide clear to land at any time. The same is true for large gatherings, but you must also not appear to be making a display flight if there are more than 1000 people there. No method of counting them comes readily to mind.

Altimeter settings
To keep within permitted airspace, you must know your height above the ground as well as your position, so an altimeter (see pages 121–126) is essential.

The altimeters we use work by measuring air pressure and translating this information into a height reading. If the air pressure were equal throughout the world, life would be very simple: altimeters could be set to the altitude of the manufacturer's factory and would not need further adjustment. Unfortunately, a change in air pressure of only one millibar will shift an altimeter's reading by about 30 ft (10 m may be easier to remember), so it is essential to be able to adjust the setting.

There are three settings you need to know about. The 'Q' code, still used for the first two, takes some getting used to:

QFE setting is when the altimeter is set to zero on the site you are operating from. Imagine you zero your altimeter, launch from a ridge and climb until it shows 300; in aviation terms you are flying at a *height* of 300 ft.

Pressure settings

Here's a practical example of why knowledge of the settings is needed: the figures are approximate.

Imagine you are flying a hill site under an airway. The height of the hill is 1,500 ft above sea level and is frankly unlikely to alter. The lower level of the airway is shown on your chart as FL40. 'Fine,' you think, 'I can climb 2,500 feet before reaching controlled airspace.' *Not necessarily.* That airway base figure will go up and down according to the Area QNH at the time. Only if that happens to be 1013.2 mb will there be 2,500 ft available to you. For each millibar that the QNH is lower, the base of the TMA will be 30 ft nearer to the hilltop. Therefore, if it is 1003.2 mb, a climb of only 2,200 ft will take you into controlled airspace. It works the other way too, so on a very high-pressure day of 1023 mb QNH you would have 2,800 ft to play with.

Once you appreciate how indicated altitudes are affected by pressure, the reason for the 'flight level' system in which all the aircraft using airways set their altimeters to the same pressure becomes obvious.

QNH setting is when the pressure adjustment of the altimeter is set to the pressure prevailing at sea level at the time and in that area (the Area QNH). If the site you are launching from is 1000 ft above sea level, on QNH setting your altimeter will show 1300 ft after a similar 300 ft climb. You are correctly described as flying at an *altitude* of 1300 ft — even though your ground clearance is only 300 ft.

The third setting, and the one you are least likely to use until you are involved in advanced cross-country flight, is Standard Pressure setting, or Pressure Altitude setting. However, you do need to know about it and to understand how it affects many of the airspace markings on the map. Here the altimeter is set to the International Standard Pressure Setting of 1013.2 mb. Aircraft using this setting are said to be at the indicated *flight level* (FL). This is the setting used by all powered aircraft once they are at a nominal 3,000 ft altitude. On the aeronautical chart, FLs are used to show the upper and lower limits of airways. They are written in multiples of one hundred feet, so FL85 means 8,500 ft as shown on an altimeter set to 1013.2 mb.

There are rules about the transition between QFE and Pressure Altitude settings, but they are beyond the scope of this book.

Temporary airspace restrictions

Certain restrictions are placed on airspace on a day-to-day basis: royal flights, with their attendant purple airways; air shows; etc. This all comes under the heading of Temporary Restricted Airspace, and in Britain you can obtain daily updates free of charge by telephoning 0500 354802.

Military Low Flying

Much British paragliding takes place in airspace shared with fast military jets flying at low level. The risk of catastrophe is reduced by using the telephone warning system which was originally set up for the use of crop sprayers but which was long ago extened to cover other air users. The free phone number is 0800 515544. Ideally, you should phone the evening before flying, but because of our unpredictable weather this is not always possible, so a morning call is still acceptable. You will need the grid reference of the site you will be taking off from, which will normally have been provided in your club's site guide. Never be shy about phoning this number: use it!

Summing up

Even if your flying is going to be restricted to ridge soaring or circuits of a tow-field, you must know if there are any limitations prevailing. If you are considering anything more ambitious, the knowledge to decipher an aeronautical chart and use the resulting information is essential.

And a final thought: an out-of-date chart is almost as useless as none at all. Each chart is revised on a one- or two-year cycle and carries an edition number, so make sure you are using the latest one. If in doubt about this, check with the appropriate department of your national aviation authority; in Britain this is the CAA Chart Room (address on page 197).

Glossary

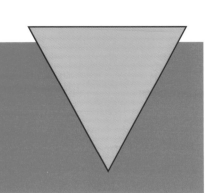

Cross-references are indicated by SMALL CAPITALS.

ACPULS System of flight testing and certification. Originally French.

AIAA Area of Intense Aerial Activity.

Airfoil (or **aerofoil**) Surface which is shaped to provide lift from moving air; in paragliding, the shape of the cross-sections of the wing chord.

Alpine launch The take-off method in which the pilot faces forwards at the start. Also called the **snatch** or **forward launch.**

AMSL Above Mean Sea Level.

Anchor-man An assistant who holds on to the pilot while the wing is being inflated in high winds.

Angle of attack The angle at which the MEAN CHORD of the airfoil meets the airflow.

ANO Air Navigation Order.

Aspect ratio The relationship between the span of the wing and its chord. A wing with a big span and a narrow chord is described as having a high aspect ratio.

ATZ Aerodrome Traffic Zone.

Backup [system] Reserve parachute.

Big ears Deliberately collapsing the tip cells of the wing to increase the rate of descent.

Blob Small weak thermal or isolated patch of lift.

Brakes Popular but slightly inaccurate term for the aerodynamic controls on a paraglider.

Camber The curve in the airfoil section. On a paraglider it can be altered by applying the brakes.

Canopy The entire fabric wing of the paraglider: the expression *wing* is normally preferred in this book.

Capewell Quick-release mechanism used by parachutists to separate from their canopies before deploying a reserve parachute. Not normally used on paragliding harnesses.

Cascade failure A series of LINE breaks resulting from progressive overload following an initial break.

Chord The measured distance between the leading and trailing edges of a wing.

CIVL Commission Internationale de Vol Libre. The international hang-gliding committee of the FAI, the governing body of both hang gliding and paragliding.

Core The area of strongest lift within a thermal. There may be several cores in a big thermal. Has produced the verb 'to core': to centre in the lift and climb efficiently.

Coriolis Force The apparent force which deflects airborne matter to the right in the northern hemisphere and to the left in the southern one. It is due to the rotation of the Earth.

Crab *see* KARABINER

Cravate A canopy deflation in which the outer part of a wing tucks under and becomes trapped in the lines, which may even loop themselves around the fabric. Cravates can be very difficult to rectify in flight — sometimes the radical solution of inducing a partial stall is the only way. The name comes from the French for necktie.

CTA Control Area.

CTR Control Zone.

FIR Flight Information Region.

FL Flight Level.

Forward launch *see* ALPINE LAUNCH

Gleitschirm German for PARAGLIDER.

Gütesiegel German flight testing and certification seal of approval.

ICAO International Civil Aviation Organization.

IMC Instrument Meteorological Conditions.

IPPI card International Pilot Proficiency Identification card. Issued by national paragliding governing bodies so that clubs and site operators in other countries can be assured of a pilot's standard.

Karabiner Connector with a quick-release gate, normally used to join the harness to the risers.

Lift band The rising air in front of a ridge which provides sufficient lift for soaring.

Lines All or any of the cords connecting wing and pilot.

Maillon Steel ring (usually rectangular) connecting the lines to a RISER. Sometimes also used instead of KARABINERS to connect the harness.

MATZ Military Aerodrome Traffic Zone.

Mean chord A line passing through the wing section via the centre of the leading edge and the trailing edge. This is the line against which the ANGLE OF ATTACK is measured.

NOTAM Notice to airmen. Official advisory notices issued by the relevant national aviation authority, and covering such things as flying displays, major competitions, NATO exercises etc. NOTAMs come in both permanent and temporary varieties.

Parachutal stall A condition in which the whole wing is stalled, but in which it retains its shape and allows the paraglider to become a parachute, with its high drag causing a vertical descent. Primitive wings designed for parascending will often do this quite safely, but higher-performance models will not.

Paraglider An aircraft which has no primary rigid structure, is capable of soaring flight and can be foot-launched from a hillside. What this book is about.

Parapente French for paraglider.

Parascending A sport closely related to paragliding, consisting of being towed into the air behind a vehicle and parachuting to the ground. Commonly used for tow-launched canopy flight of a non-soaring nature.

PLF Parachute Landing Fall.

Polar [curve] A graph plotting the sink rate of a glider throughout its speed range.

Porosity The property of a material that allows air to pass through it. For paraglider cloth, the lower the porosity, the better.

Pumping Pulling BRAKES to re-inflate a partially collapsed wing.

PWC Paragliding World Cup annual competition series.

Rescue [system] The expression commonly used in Europe for the BACKUP or reserve parachute.

Reserve *see* BACKUP

Risers The lengths of webbing between the harness and the LINES. Will be designated A-risers, B-risers etc, according to the set of lines to which they are attached.

Rotor Air turbulence caused by a large obstacle — usually a ridge or range of mountains.

Scratching Flying close to the ground in light lift.

Shooting The tendency for a canopy to surge forwards when recovering from a stall or during initial inflation.

SIV *Simulation d'incidente en vol.* Usually a course in which canopy collapses, spins and other potential disasters are practised safely, over water.

Snatch *see* ALPINE LAUNCH

Stall Sudden loss of lift due to breakup of orderly airflow over the wing.

TMA Terminal Manoeuvring Area.

Toggle The word used by parachutists for the handles on the control lines. Hence **toggling** is sometimes used to describe steering.

Trim speed The speed at which the paraglider flies 'hands-off'.

Tuck Wing collapse caused by the leading edge collapsing downwards and closing the front of the cells.

V-lines Another name for RISERS.

VFR Visual Flight Rules.

VMC Visual Meteorological Conditions. To be in VMC you must remain 1000 ft vertically clear of cloud and 1,500 metres clear horizontally, and there must be a flight visibility of 8 km.

Window The time period available for launching.

Wing *see* CANOPY

Wraps Temporarily shortening the brake lines by looping them around your hands. Potentially risky in flight, but useful when ground-handling or just before making a nil-wind landing.

XC Cross-country flight.

Further reading

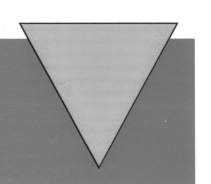

Books

The books listed here are published in the United Kingdom except where otherwise indicated.

Aviation law for applicants for the Private Pilot's Licence[CAP 85], CAA Publications, 1992

Tom Bradbury, *Meteorology and Flight*, A & C Black, 1989

Ian Currer and Rob Cruickshank, *Touching Cloudbase*, Leading Edge, 1996

Dennis Pagen, *Understanding the Sky*, Sports Aviation Publications (USA), n.d.

Derek Piggott, *Understanding Flying Weather*, A & C Black, 1988

David Sollom and Matthew Cook, *Paragliding from beginner to cross-country*, Crowood Press, 1998

C. E. Wallington, *Meteorology for Glider Pilots*, John Murray, 1977 (out of print)

Alan Watts, *Air Rider's Weather*, A & C Black, 1992

Noel Whittall, *Paramotoring from the ground up*, Airlife, 2000

Magazines

Cross-Country
(France, but printed in English)

Delta & Parapendio
(Italy)

Drachenflieger
(Germany)

Para World
(Japan)

Paragliding — The Magazine
(USA)

Swiss Glider
(Switzerland, printed in French and German)

Skywings
(UK)
The BHPA magazine

Vol Libre
(France)

Useful addresses

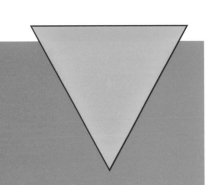

British Hang Gliding and
  Paragliding Association Ltd
The Old Schoolroom
Loughborough Road
Leicester
LE4 5PJ
Tel: 0116 261 1322
Fax: 0116 261 1323
e-mail: office@bhpa.co.uk

CAA charts distributed by:
Westward Digital Ltd
37 Windsor Street
Cheltenham
Gloucestershire
GL52 2DG
Tel: 01242 235151
Fax: 01242 584139

Hang Gliding Federation of
  Australia
P O Box 558
Tumut
NSW 2720
Australia
Tel: +61 2 69 472 888
Fax: +61 2 69 474 328
e-mail: hgfa@tpgi.com.au

Hang Gliding and Paragliding
  Association of Canada
#13 13670 84 Ave.
Surrey
British Columbia
Canada
V3W 0T6
Tel: +1 604 507 2565
Fax: +1 604 507 2565

Fédération Aéronautique
  Internationale
Avenue Mon Repos 24
1005 Lausanne
Switzerland
Tel: +41 21 345 1070
Fax: +41 21 345 1077
e-mail: office@fai.org

New Zealand Hang-Gliding
  and Paragliding Association
  Inc.
P O Box 3521
Richmond
Nelson
New Zealand
Tel: +64 3 540 2183
Fax: +64 3 540 2183
e-mail:
  nzhgpa.admins@clear.net.nz

South African Hang Gliding
  and Paragliding Association
P O Box 1993
Halfway House
1685
South Africa
Tel: +27 11 805 5429
Fax: +27 11 805 5429
e-mail:
  sahpa@paragliding.co.za

United States Hang Gliding
  Association
P O Box 8300
Colorado Springs
CO 80933
USA
Tel: +1 719 632 8300
Fax: +1 719 632 6417
e-mail: ushga@ushga.org

Index

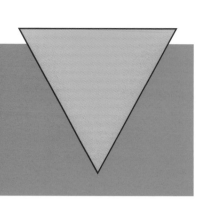